What It Takes

Academic Writing in College

SECOND EDITION

Laurence Behrens
*University of California,
Santa Barbara*

Leonard J. Rosen
Bentley University

Boston   Columbus   Indianapolis   New York   San Francisco
Upper Saddle River   Amsterdam   Cape Town   Dubai   London   Madrid
Milan   Munich   Paris   Montréal   Toronto   Delhi   Mexico City
São Paulo   Sydney   Hong Kong   Seoul
Singapore   Taipei   Tokyo

Senior Acquisitions Editor: Brad Potthoff
Senior Marketing Manager: Sandra McGuire
Project Coordination, Text Design, and Electronic Page Makeup: Kailash Jadli/Aptara®, Inc.
Cover Director: Jayne Conte
Designer: Suzanne Duda
Cover Image: Shutterstock
Photo Researcher: Stefanie Ramsey
Production Manager: Pat Brown
Printer and Binder: Courier Companies, Inc.
Cover Printer: Courier Companies, Inc.

Credits and acknowledgements borrowed from other sources and reproduced, with permission, in this textbook appear on page 172.

Library of Congress Cataloging-in-Publication Data

Behrens, Laurence
  What it takes : academic writing in college / Laurence Behrens, Leonard Rosen. — 2nd ed.
    p. cm.
  Includes bibliographical references and index.
  Originally published as what it takes: writing in college.
  ISBN-13: 978-0-205-86484-3
  ISBN-10: 0-205-86484-8
  1. English language—Rhetoric—Problems, exercises, etc.   2. Report writing—Problems, exercises, etc.   3. Critical thinking—Problems, exercises, etc.   4. College readers.   I. Rosen, Leonard J.   II. Title.
  PE1408.B46928 2012
  808'.042—dc23

                                                    2012017938

11   17

PEARSON

ISBN-10:   0-205-86484-8
ISBN-13: 978-0-205-86484-3

Detailed Contents

Preface

What It Takes: Writing in College addresses four core skills that students should master to succeed as writers in college: the *summary*, the *critique*, the *synthesis*, and the *analysis.* The material here, in abbreviated form, constitutes the first part of *our Writing and Reading Across the Curriculum.* Over the past 30 years this text has helped writers new to academic settings to work with source materials and to generate competent, evidence-based papers across the disciplines.

Much of academic writing involves argument. Accordingly, *What It Takes* emphasizes the following:

- **The Elements of Argument: Claim, Support, and Assumption.** This section adapts the Toulmin approach to argument to the kinds of readings that students typically encounter when conducting research for their papers.

- **Developing and Organizing the Support for Your Arguments.** This section helps students to mine source materials for facts, expert opinions, and examples that will support their arguments.

- **Annotated Student Argument Paper.** A sample student paper highlights and discusses argumentative strategies that a student uses in drafting and developing a paper.

Throughout the text, we include boxed material that emphasizes the practical applications of writing summaries, syntheses, critiques, and analyses. The chapters are organized as follows:

Chapter 1: Summary

Students are taken through the process of writing a summary of Alan S. Blinder's "Will Your Job be Exported?"—an economist's glimpse into the future of the global work force and the stability of American jobs. (Expect to be surprised.) We demonstrate how to annotate a source and divide it into sections, how to develop a thesis, and how to write and smoothly join section summaries.

Chapter 2: Critical Reading and Critique

Chapter 2 offers a model critique on "The Moon We Left Behind" by Charles Krauthammer, an op-ed that argues against the cancellation of the manned space program. The critique follows a set of guidelines for practicing critical reading.

Chapter 3: Synthesis

Chapter 3 provides an argument synthesis on the topic of student privacy vs. campus safety in the wake of the Virginia Tech shootings. The argument synthesizes opinion pieces, newspaper and magazine articles, federal law, and an important investigative panel report. This section is followed by an example comparison-contrast synthesis, framed as a response to an exam question on World War I and World War II. The chapter concludes with excerpts from an explanatory synthesis on the subject of student privacy vs. campus safety, illustrating the differences between argumentation and explanation.

Chapter 4: Analysis

The analysis chapter opens with brief, competing analyses of *The Wizard of Oz* that demonstrate how, employing different analytical principles (one psychoanalytic and the other political), two writers can read very different meanings into the classic children's book and movie. Following an example analysis by Marie Winn that examines excessive television viewing as an addiction ("The Plug-In Drug"), we present a student example of analysis: an application of a theory by sociologist Robert H. Knapp to a widespread rumor about unsuspecting travelers having their kidneys surgically removed. We explain how to locate principles useful for conducting analyses, and we show how to write analyses themselves.

A Note to the Student

Your sociology professor asks you to write a paper on attitudes toward the homeless population of an urban area near your campus. You are expected to consult books, articles, Web sites, and other online sources on the subject, and you are also encouraged to conduct surveys and interviews.

Your professor is making a number of assumptions about your capabilities. Among them:

- that you can research and assess the value of relevant sources;
- that you can comprehend college-level material, both print and electronic;
- that you can use theories and principles learned from one set of sources as tools to investigate other sources (or events, people, places, or things);
- that you can synthesize separate but related sources;
- that you can intelligently respond to such material.

These same assumptions underlie practically all college writing assignments. Your professors will expect you to demonstrate that you can read and understand not only textbooks but also critical articles and books, primary sources, Internet sources, online academic databases, and other material related to a particular subject of study. For example: For a paper on the progress of the Human Genome Project, you would probably look to articles and Internet sources for the most recent information. Using an online database, you would find articles on the subject in such print journals as *Nature, Journal of the American Medical Association,* and *Bioscience,* as well as in leading newspapers and magazines. A Web search engine might lead you to a useful site called "A New Gene Map of the Human Genome" <http://www.ncbi.nlm.nih.gov/genemap99/> and the site of the "Sequencing" section of the U.S. Department of Energy Joint Genome Institute <http://www.jgi/doe/gov/sequencing/index/html>. You would be expected to assess the relevance of such sources to your topic and to draw from them the information and ideas you need. It's even possible that the final product of your research and reading may not be a conventional paper at all, but rather a Web site you create that explains the science behind the Human Genome Project, explores a particular controversy about the project, or describes the future benefits geneticists hope to derive from the project.

For a different class, you might be assigned a research paper on the films of the director Martin Scorsese. To get started, you might consult your film studies textbook, biographical sources on Scorsese, and anthologies of criticism. Instructor and peer feedback on a first draft might lead you to articles in both popular magazines (such as *Time*) and scholarly journals (such as *Literature/Film Quarterly*), a CD-ROM database (such as *Film Index International*), and relevant Web sites (such as the "Internet Movie Database" <http://us.imdb.com>).

These two assignment examples are very different, but the skills you need to work with them are the same. You must be able to research relevant sources. You must be able to read and comprehend those sources. You must be able to perceive the relationships among several pieces of source material. And you must be able to apply your own critical judgment to these various materials.

What It Takes: Writing in College provides you with the opportunity to practice the essential college-level skills we have just outlined and the forms of writing associated with them: the *summary*, the *critique*, the *synthesis*, and the *analysis*.

We hope that your writing course will serve as a kind of bridge to your other courses and that as a result of this work you will become more skillful at perceiving and expressing relationships among diverse topics. This little book can help you along your way. Because it involves such critical and widely applicable skills, your writing course may well turn out to be the most valuable—and one of the most interesting—of your academic career.

Laurence Behrens
Leonard J. Rosen

1

Summary

WHAT IS A SUMMARY?

The best way to demonstrate that you understand the information and the ideas in any piece of writing is to compose an accurate and clearly written summary of that piece. By a *summary* we mean a brief restatement, *in your own words, of the content of a passage* (a group of paragraphs, a chapter, an article, a book). This restatement should focus on the *central idea* of the passage. The briefest of summaries (one or two sentences) will do no more than this. A longer, more complete summary will indicate, in condensed form, the main points in the passage that support or explain the central idea. It will reflect the order in which these points are presented and the emphasis given to them. It may even include some important examples from the passage. But it will not include minor details. It will not repeat points simply for the purpose of emphasis. And it will not contain any of your own opinions or conclusions. A good summary, therefore, has three central qualities: *brevity, completeness*, and *objectivity*.

CAN A SUMMARY BE OBJECTIVE?

Objectivity could be difficult to achieve in a summary. By definition, writing a summary requires you to select some aspects of the original and leave out others. Since deciding what to select and what to leave out calls for your judgment, your summary really is a work of interpretation. And, certainly, your interpretation of a passage may differ from another person's.

One factor affecting the nature and quality of your interpretation is your *prior knowledge* of the subject. For example, if you're attempting to summarize an anthropological article and you're a novice in that field, then your summary of the article will likely differ from that of your professor, who has spent twenty years studying this particular area and whose judgment about what is more or less significant is undoubtedly more reliable than your own. By the same token, your personal or professional *frame of reference* may also affect your interpretation. A union representative and a management representative attempting to summarize the latest management offer would probably come up with two very different accounts. Still, we believe that in most cases it's possible to produce a reasonably objective summary of a passage if you make a conscious, good-faith effort to be unbiased and to prevent your own feelings on the subject from coloring your account of the author's text.

USING THE SUMMARY

In some quarters, the summary has a bad reputation—and with reason. Summaries are often provided by writers as substitutes for analyses. As students, many of us have summarized books that we were supposed to *review critically.* All the same, the summary does have a place in respectable college work. First, writing a summary is an excellent way to understand what you read. This in itself is an important goal of academic study. If you don't understand your source material, chances are you won't be able to refer to it usefully in a paper. Summaries help you understand what you read because they force you to put the text into your own words. Practice with writing summaries also develops your general writing habits, because a good summary, like any other piece of good writing, is clear, coherent, and accurate.

Second, summaries are useful to your readers. Let's say you're writing a paper about the McCarthy era in the United States, and in part of that paper you want to discuss Arthur Miller's *The Crucible* as a dramatic treatment of the subject. A summary of the plot would be helpful to a reader who hasn't seen or read—or who doesn't remember—the play. Or

WHERE DO WE FIND WRITTEN SUMMARIES?

Here are just a few of the types of writing that involve summary:

Academic Writing

- **Critique papers** summarize material in order to critique it.
- **Synthesis papers** summarize to show relationships between sources.
- **Analysis papers** summarize theoretical perspectives before applying them.
- **Research papers** require note taking that summarize the content of source materials.
- **Literature reviews** summarize currents research on a topic.
- **Argument papers** summarize evidence and opposing arguments.
- **Essay exams** demonstrate understanding of course materials through summary.

Workplace Writing

- **Policy briefs** condense complex public policy.
- **Business plans** summarize costs, relevant environmental impacts, and other important matters.
- **Memos, letters, and reports** summarize procedures, meetings, product assessments, expenditures, and more.
- **Medical charts** record patient data in summarized form.
- **Legal briefs** summarize relevant facts and arguments of cases.

perhaps you're writing a paper about the politics of recent American military interventions. If your reader isn't likely to be familiar with American actions in Kosovo and Afghanistan, it would be a good idea to summarize these events at some early point in the paper. In many cases (an exam, for instance), you can use a summary to demonstrate your knowledge of what your professor already knows; when writing a paper, you can use a summary to inform your professor about some relatively unfamiliar source.

Third, summaries are required frequently in college-level writing. For example, on a psychology midterm, you may be asked to explain Carl Jung's theory of the collective unconscious and to show how it differs from Sigmund Freud's theory of the personal unconscious. You may have read about Jung's theory in your textbook or in a supplementary article, or your instructor may have outlined it in her lecture. You can best demonstrate your understanding of it by summarizing it. Then you'll proceed to contrast it with Freud's theory—which, of course, you must also summarize.

THE READING PROCESS

It may seem to you that being able to tell (or retell) in summary form exactly what a passage says is a skill that ought to be taken for granted in anyone who can read at high school level. Unfortunately, this is not so: For all kinds of reasons, people don't always read carefully. In fact, it's probably safe to say that usually they don't. Either they read so inattentively that they skip over words, phrases, or even whole sentences, or, if they do see the words in front of them, they see them without registering their significance.

When a reader fails to pick up the meaning and implications of a sentence or two, usually there's no real harm done. (An exception: You could lose credit on an exam or paper because you failed to read or to realize the significance of a crucial direction by your instructor.) But over longer stretches—the paragraph, the section, the article, or the chapter—inattentive or haphazard reading interferes with your goals as a reader: to perceive the shape of the argument, to grasp the central idea, to determine the main points that compose it, to relate the parts of the whole, and to note key examples. This kind of reading takes a lot more energy and determination than casual reading. But in the long run, it's an energy-saving method because it enables you to retain the content of the material and to draw upon that content in your own responses. In other words, it allows you to develop an accurate and coherent written discussion that goes beyond summary.

CRITICAL READING FOR SUMMARY

- *Examine the context.* Note the credentials, occupation, and publications of the author. Identify the source in which the piece originally appeared. This information helps illuminate the author's perspective on the topic he or she is addressing.
- *Note the title and subtitle.* Some titles are straightforward; the meanings of others become clearer as you read. In either case, titles typically identify the topic being addressed and often reveal the author's attitude toward that topic.
- *Identify the main point.* Whether a piece of writing contains a thesis statement in the first few paragraphs or builds its main point without stating it up front, look at the entire piece to arrive at an understanding of the overall point being made.
- *Identify the subordinate points.* Notice the smaller subpoints that make up the main point, and make sure you understand how they relate to the main point. If a particular subpoint doesn't clearly relate to the main point you've identified, you may need to modify your understanding of the main point.
- *Break the reading into sections.* Notice which paragraphs make up a piece's introduction, body, and conclusion. Break up the body paragraphs into sections that address the writer's various subpoints.
- *Distinguish between points, examples, and counterarguments.* Critical reading requires careful attention to what a writer is *doing* as well as what he or she is *saying.*

(Continued on next page)

When a writer quotes someone else, or relays an example of something, ask yourself why this is being done. What point is the example supporting? Is another source being quoted as support for a point or as a counterargument that the writer sets out to address?

- *Watch for transitions within and between paragraphs.* In order to follow the logic of a piece of writing, as well as to distinguish between points, examples, and counterarguments, pay attention to the transitional words and phrases writers use. Transitions function like road signs, preparing the reader for what's next.

- *Read actively and recursively.* Don't treat reading as a passive, linear progression through a text. Instead, read as though you are engaged in a dialogue with the writer: Ask questions of the text as you read, make notes in the margin, underline key ideas in pencil, put question or exclamation marks next to passages that confuse or excite you. Go back to earlier points once you finish a reading, stop during your reading to recap what's come so far, and move back and forth through a text.

HOW TO WRITE SUMMARIES

Every article you read will present its own challenge as you work to summarize it. As you'll discover, saying in a few words what has taken someone else a great many can be difficult. But like any other skill, the ability to summarize improves with practice. Here are a few pointers to get you started. They represent possible stages, or steps, in the process of writing a summary. These pointers are not meant to be iron-clad rules; rather, they are designed to encourage habits of thinking that will allow you to vary your technique as the situation demands.

GUIDELINES FOR WRITING SUMMARIES

- *Read the passage carefully.* Determine its structure. Identify the author's purpose in writing. (This will help you distinguish between more important and less important information.) Make a note in the margin when you get confused or when you think something is important; highlight or underline points sparingly, if at all.

- *Reread.* This time divide the passage into sections or stages of thought. The author's use of paragraphing will often be a useful guide. *Label,* on the passage itself, each section or stage of thought. *Underline* key ideas and terms. Write notes in the margin.

- *Write one-sentence summaries,* on a separate sheet of paper, of each stage of thought.

- *Write a thesis—a one- or two-sentence summary of the entire passage.* The thesis should express the central idea of the passage, as you have determined it from the preceding steps. You may find it useful to follow the approach of most newspaper stories—naming the *what, who, why, where, when,* and *how* of the matter. For persuasive passages, summarize in a sentence the author's conclusion. For descriptive passages, indicate the subject of the description and its key feature(s). *Note:* In some cases, *a suitable thesis statement may already be in the original passage.* If so, you may want to quote it directly in your summary.

- *Write the first draft of your summary* by (1) combining the thesis with your list of one-sentence summaries or (2) combining the thesis with one-sentence summaries *plus* significant details from the passage. In either case, eliminate repetition and less important information. Disregard minor details or generalize them (e.g., Bill Clinton and George W. Bush might be generalized as "recent presidents"). Use as few words as possible to convey the main ideas.

(Continued on next page)

- *Check your summary against the original passage* and make whatever adjustments are necessary for accuracy and completeness.
- *Revise your summary,* inserting transitional words and phrases where necessary to ensure coherence. Check for style. *Avoid a series of short, choppy sentences.* Combine sentences for a smooth, logical flow of ideas. Check for grammatical correctness, punctuation, and spelling.

DEMONSTRATION: SUMMARY

To demonstrate these points at work, let's go through the process of summarizing a passage of expository material—that is, writing that is meant to inform and/or persuade. Read the following selection carefully. Try to identify its parts and understand how they work together to create an overall statement.

Will Your Job Be Exported?

Alan S. Blinder

Alan S. Blinder is the Gordon S. Rentschler Memorial Professor of Economics at Princeton University. He has served as vice chairman of the Federal Reserve Board and was a member of President Clinton's original Council of Economic Advisers.

1   The great conservative political philosopher Edmund Burke, who probably would not have been a reader of *The American Prospect,* once observed, "You can never plan the future by the past."[1] But when it comes to preparing the American workforce for the jobs of the future, we may be doing just that.

---

[1]Edmund Burke (1729–1797) was a conservative British statesman, philosopher, and author. *The American Prospect,* in which "Will Your Job Be Exported?" first appeared in the November 2006 issue, describes itself as "an authoritative magazine of liberal ideas."

2   For about a quarter-century, demand for labor appears to have shifted toward the college-educated and away from high school graduates and dropouts. This shift, most economists believe, is the primary (though not the sole) reason for rising income inequality, and there is no end in sight. Economists refer to this phenomenon by an antiseptic name: skill-biased technical progress. In plain English, it means that the labor market has turned ferociously against the low skilled and the uneducated.

3   In a progressive society, such a worrisome social phenomenon might elicit some strong policy responses, such as more compensatory education, stepped-up efforts at retraining, reinforcement (rather than shredding) of the social safety net, and so on. You don't fight the market's valuation of skills; you try to mitigate its more deleterious effects. We did a bit of this in the United States in the 1990s, by raising the minimum wage and expanding the Earned Income Tax Credit.[2] Combined with tight labor markets, these measures improved things for the average worker. But in this decade, little or no mitigation has been attempted. Social Darwinism has come roaring back.[3]

4   With one big exception: We have expended considerable efforts to keep more young people in school longer (e.g., reducing high-school dropouts and sending more kids to college) and to improve the quality of schooling (e.g., via charter schools and No Child Left Behind[4]). Success in these domains may have been modest, but not for lack of

---

[2]The Earned Income Tax Credit, an anti-poverty measure enacted by Congress in 1975 and revised in the 1980s and 1990s, provides a credit against federal income taxes for any filer who claims a dependent child.

[3]Social Darwinism, a largely discredited philosophy dating from the Victorian era and espoused by Herbert Spenser, asserts that Charles Darwin's observations on natural selection apply to human societies. Social Darwinists argue that the poor are less fit to survive than the wealthy and should, through a natural process of adaptation, be allowed to die out.

[4]Charter schools are public schools with specialized missions to operate outside of regulations that some feel restrict creativity and performance in traditional school settings. The No Child Left Behind Act of 2001 (NCLB) mandates standards-based education for all schools receiving federal funding. Both the charter schools movement and NCLB can be understood as efforts to improve public education.

trying. You don't have to remind Americans that education is important; the need for educational reform is etched into the public consciousness. Indeed, many people view education as the silver bullet. On hearing the question "How do we best prepare the American workforce of the future?" many Americans react reflexively with: "Get more kids to study science and math, and send more of them to college."

5   Which brings me to the future. As I argued in a recent article in *Foreign Affairs* magazine, the greatest problem for the next generation of American workers may not be lack of education, but rather "offshoring"—the movement of jobs overseas, especially to countries with much lower wages, such as India and China. Manufacturing jobs have been migrating overseas for decades. But the new wave of offshoring, of *service* jobs, is something different.

6   Traditionally, we think of service jobs as being largely immune to foreign competition. After all, you can't get your hair cut by a barber or your broken arm set by a doctor in a distant land. But stunning advances in communication technology, plus the emergence of a vast new labor pool in Asia and Eastern Europe, are changing that picture radically, subjecting millions of presumed-safe domestic service jobs to foreign competition. And it is not necessary actually to move jobs to low-wage countries in order to restrain wage increases; the mere threat of offshoring can put a damper on wages.

7   Service-sector offshoring is a minor phenomenon so far, Lou Dobbs notwithstanding; probably well under 1 percent of U.S. service jobs have been outsourced.[5] But I believe that service-sector offshoring will eventually exceed manufacturing-sector offshoring by a hefty margin—for three main reasons. The first is simple arithmetic: There are vastly more service jobs than manufacturing jobs in the United States (and in other rich countries). Second, the technological advances that have made service-sector offshoring possible will continue

---

[5]Lou Dobbs, a conservative columnist and former political commentator for CNN, is well known for his anti-immigration views.

and accelerate, so the range of services that can be moved offshore will increase ineluctably. Third, the number of (e.g., Indian and Chinese) workers capable of performing service jobs offshore seems certain to grow, perhaps exponentially.

8   I do not mean to paint a bleak picture here. Ever since Adam Smith and David Ricardo, economists have explained and extolled the gains in living standards that derive from international trade.[6] Those arguments are just as valid for trade in services as for trade in goods. There really *are* net gains to the United States from expanding service-sector trade with India, China, and the rest. The offshoring problem is not about the adverse nature of what economists call the economy's eventual equilibrium. Rather, it is about the so-called transition—the ride from here to there. That ride, which could take a generation or more, may be bumpy. And during the long adjustment period, many U.S. wages could face downward pressure.

9   Thus far, only American manufacturing workers and a few low-end service workers (e.g., call-center operators) have been competing, at least potentially, with millions of people in faraway lands eager to work for what seems a pittance by U.S. standards. But offshoring is no longer limited to low-end service jobs. Computer code can be written overseas and e-mailed back to the United States. So can your tax return and lots of legal work, provided you do not insist on face-to-face contact with the accountant or lawyer. In writing and editing this article, I communicated with the editors and staff of *The American Prospect* only by telephone and e-mail. Why couldn't they (or I, for that matter) have been in India? The possibilities are, if not endless, at least vast.

10   What distinguishes the jobs that cannot be offshored from the ones that can? The crucial distinction is not—and

---

[6]Adam Smith (1723–1790), Scottish author of *An Inquiry into the Nature and Causes of the Wealth of Nations* (1776), established the foundations of modern economics. David Ricardo (1772–1823) was a British businessman, statesman, and economist who founded the classical school of economics and is best known for his studies of monetary policy.

this is the central point of this essay—the required levels of skill and education. These attributes have been critical to labor-market success in the past, but may be less so in the future. Instead, the new critical distinction may be that some services either require personal delivery (e.g., driving a taxi and brain surgery) or are seriously degraded when delivered electronically (e.g., college teaching—at least, I hope!), while other jobs (e.g., call centers and keyboard data entry) are not. Call the first category personal services and the second category impersonal services. With this terminology, I have three main points to make about preparing our workforce for the brave, new world of the future.

11   First, we need to think about, plan, and redesign our educational system with the crucial distinction between personal service jobs and impersonal service jobs in mind. Many of the impersonal service jobs will migrate offshore, but the personal service jobs will stay here.

12   Second, the line that divides personal services from impersonal services will move in only one direction over time, as technological progress makes it possible to deliver an ever-increasing array of services electronically.

13   Third, the novel distinction between personal and impersonal jobs is quite different from, and appears essentially unrelated to, the traditional distinction between jobs that do and do not require high levels of education.

14   For example, it is easy to offshore working in a call center, typing transcripts, writing computer code, and reading X-rays. The first two require little education; the last two require quite a lot. On the other hand, it is either impossible or very difficult to offshore janitorial services, fast-food restaurant service, college teaching, and open-heart surgery. Again, the first two occupations require little or no education, while the last two require a great deal. There seems to be little or no correlation between educational requirements (the old concern) and how "offshorable" jobs are (the new one).

15   If so, the implications could be startling. A generation from now, civil engineers (who must be physically present) may

be in greater demand in the United States than computer engineers (who don't). Similarly, there might be more divorce lawyers (not offshorable) than tax lawyers (partly offshorable). More imaginatively, electricians might earn more than computer programmers. I am not predicting any of this; lots of things influence relative demands and supplies for different types of labor. But it all seems within the realm of the possible as technology continues to enhance the offshorability of even highly skilled occupations. What does seem highly likely is that the relative demand for labor in the United States will shift away from impersonal services and toward personal services, and this shift will look quite different from the familiar story of skill-biased technical progress. So Burke's warning is worth heeding.

16   I am *not* suggesting that education will become a handicap in the job market of the future. On the contrary, to the extent that education raises productivity and that better-educated workers are more adaptable and/or more creative, a wage premium for higher education should remain. Thus, it still makes sense to send more of America's youth to college. But, over the next generation, the kind of education our young people receive may prove to be more important than how much education they receive. In that sense, a college degree may lose its exalted "silver bullet" status.

17   Looking back over the past 25 years, "stay in school longer" was excellent advice for success in the labor market. But looking forward over the next 25 years, more subtle occupational advice may be needed. "Prepare yourself for a high-end personal service occupation that is not offshorable" is a more nuanced message than "stay in school." But it may prove to be more useful. And many non-offshorable jobs—such as carpenters, electricians, and plumbers—do not require college education.

18   The hard question is how to make this more subtle advice concrete and actionable. The children entering America's educational system today, at age 5, will emerge into a very different labor market when they leave it. Given gestation periods of 13 to 17 years and more, educators and policy-makers need

to be thinking now about the kinds of training and skills that will best prepare these children for their future working lives. Specifically, it is essential to educate America's youth for the jobs that will actually be available in America 20 to 30 years from now, not for the jobs that will have moved offshore.

19   Some of the personal service jobs that will remain in the United States will be very high-end (doctors), others will be less glamorous though well paid (plumbers), and some will be "dead end" (janitor). We need to think long and hard about the types of skills that best prepare people to deliver high-end personal services, and how to teach those skills in our elementary and high schools. I am not an education specialist, but it strikes me that, for example, the central thrust of No Child Left Behind is pushing the nation in exactly the wrong direction. I am all for accountability. But the nation's school system will not build the creative, flexible, people-oriented workforce we will need in the future by drilling kids incessantly with rote preparation for standardized tests in the vain hope that they will perform as well as memory chips.

20   Starting in the elementary schools, we need to develop our youngsters' imaginations and people skills as well as their "reading, writing, and 'rithmetic." Remember that kindergarten grade for "works and plays well with others"? It may become increasingly important in a world of personally delivered services. Such training probably needs to be continued and made more sophisticated in the secondary schools, where, for example, good communications skills need to be developed.

21   More vocational education is probably also in order. After all, nurses, carpenters, and plumbers are already scarce, and we'll likely need more of them in the future. Much vocational training now takes place in community colleges; and they, too, need to adapt their curricula to the job market of the future.

22   While it is probably still true that we should send more kids to college and increase the number who study science, math, and engineering, we need to focus on training more college students for the high-end jobs that are unlikely to move offshore, and on developing a creative workforce that will keep America incubating and developing new processes,

new products, and entirely new industries. Offshoring is, after all, mostly about following and copying. America needs to lead and innovate instead, just as we have in the past.

23   Educational reform is not the whole story, of course. I suggested at the outset, for example, that we needed to repair our tattered social safety net and turn it into a retraining trampoline that bounces displaced workers back into productive employment. But many low-end personal service jobs cannot be turned into more attractive jobs simply by more training—think about janitors, fast-food workers, and nurse's aides, for example. Running a tight labor market would help such workers, as would a higher minimum wage, an expanded Earned Income Tax Credit, universal health insurance, and the like.

24   Moving up the skill ladder, employment is concentrated in the public or quasi-public sector in a number of service occupations. Teachers and health-care workers are two prominent examples. In such cases, government policy can influence wages and working conditions directly by upgrading the structure and pay of such jobs—developing more professional early-childhood teachers and fewer casual daycare workers for example—as long as the taxpayer is willing to foot the bill. Similarly, some service jobs such as registered nurses are in short supply mainly because we are not training enough qualified personnel. Here, too, public policy can help by widening the pipeline to allow more workers through. So there are a variety of policy levers that might do some good—if we are willing to pull them.

25   But all that said, education is still the right place to start. Indeed, it is much more than that because the educational system affects the entire population and because no other institution is nearly as important when it comes to preparing our youth for the world of work. As the first industrial revolution took hold, America radically transformed (and democratized) its educational system to meet the new demands of an industrial society. We may need to do something like that again. There is a great deal at stake here. If we get this one wrong, the next generation will pay dearly. But if we get it

(close to) right, the gains from trade promise coming generations a prosperous future.

26   The somewhat inchoate challenge posed here—preparing more young Americans for personal service jobs—brings to mind one of my favorite Churchill quotations: "You can always count on Americans to do the right thing—after they've tried everything else." It is time to start trying.

Read, Reread, Highlight

Let's consider our recommended pointers for writing a summary.

As you reread the passage, note in the margins of the essay important points, shifts in thought, and questions you may have. Consider the essay's significance as a whole and its stages of thought. What does it say? How is it organized? How does each part of the passage fit into the whole? What do all these points add up to?

Here is how several paragraphs from the middle of Blinder's article might look after you have marked the main ideas by highlighting and by marginal notations.

Service-sector offshoring is a minor phenomenon so far, Lou Dobbs notwithstanding; probably well under 1 percent of U.S. service jobs have been outsourced. But I believe that

Offshored service jobs will eclipse lost manufacturing jobs—3 reasons

service-sector offshoring will eventually exceed manufacturing-sector offshoring by a hefty margin—for three main reasons. The first is simple arithmetic: There are vastly more service jobs than manufacturing jobs in the United States (and in other rich countries). Second, the technological advances that have made service-sector offshoring possible will continue and accelerate, so the range of services that can be moved offshore will increase ineluctably. Third, the number of (e.g., Indian and Chinese) workers capable of performing service jobs offshore seems certain to grow, perhaps exponentially.

I do not mean to paint a bleak picture here. Ever since Adam Smith and David Ricardo, economists have

Long-term economy will be ok. Short-to-middle term will be "bumpy"

explained and extolled the gains in living standards that derive from international trade. Those arguments are just as valid for trade in services as for trade in goods. There really are net gains to the United States from expanding service-sector trade with India, China, and the rest. The offshoring problem is not about the adverse nature of what economists call the economy's eventual equilibrium. Rather, it is about the so-called transition—the ride from here to there. That ride, which could take a generation or more, may be bumpy. And during the long adjustment period, many U.S. wages could face downward pressure.

Thus far, only American manufacturing workers and a few low-end service workers (e.g., call-center operators) have been competing, at least potentially, with millions of people in faraway lands eager to work for what seems a pittance by U.S. standards. But offshoring is no longer limited to low-end service jobs. Computer code can be written overseas and e-mailed back to the United States. So can your tax return and lots of legal work, provided you do not insist on face-to-face contact with the accountant or lawyer. In writing and editing this article, I communicated with the editors and staff of *The American Prospect* only by telephone and e-mail. Why couldn't they (or I, for that matter) have been in India? The possibilities are, if not endless, at least vast.

High-end jobs to be lost

What distinguishes the jobs that cannot be offshored from the ones that can? The crucial distinction is not—and this is the central point of this essay—the required levels of skill and education. These attributes have been critical to labor-market success in the past, but may be less so in the future. Instead, the new critical distinction may be that some services either require personal delivery (e.g., driving a taxi and brain surgery) or are seriously degraded when delivered electronically (e.g., college teaching—at least, I hope!), while other jobs (e.g., call centers and keyboard data entry) are not. Call the first category personal services and the second category impersonal services. With this terminology, I have three main points to make about preparing our workforce for the brave, new world of the future.

B's main point: Key distinction: Personal Service jobs stay; impersonal jobs go

3 points re:
prep of
future work-
force

First, we need to think about, plan, and redesign our educational system with the crucial distinction between personal service jobs and impersonal service jobs in mind. Many of the impersonal service jobs will migrate offshore, but the personal service jobs will stay here.

Movement:
impersonal
→ personal

Second, the line that divides personal services from impersonal services will move in only one direction over time, as technological progress makes it possible to deliver an ever-increasing array of services electronically.

Level of ed.
not related
to future
job security

Third, the novel distinction between personal and impersonal jobs is quite different from, and appears essentially unrelated to, the traditional distinction between jobs that do and do not require high levels of education.

Divide into Stages of Thought

When a selection doesn't contain sections with thematic headings, as is the case with "Will Your Job Be Exported?", how do you determine where one stage of thought ends and the next one begins? Assuming that what you have read is coherent and unified, this should not be difficult. (When a selection is unified, all of its parts pertain to the main subject; when a selection is coherent, the parts follow one another in logical order.) Look particularly for transitional sentences at the beginning of paragraphs. Such sentences generally work in one or both of two ways: (1) they summarize what has come before; (2) they set the stage for what is to follow.

Look at the sentences that open paragraphs 5 and 10: "Which brings me to the future" and "What distinguishes the jobs that cannot be offshored from the ones that can?" In both cases, Blinder makes a clear announcement. Grammatically speaking, "Which brings me to the future" is a fragment, not a sentence. Experienced writers will use fragments on occasion to good effect, as in this case. The fragment clearly has the sense of a complete thought: the pronoun "which" refers readers to the content of the preceding paragraphs, asking readers to summarize that content and then, with the predicate "brings me to the future," to move forward into the next part of the article. Similarly, the question "What distinguishes the jobs that cannot be offshored from the ones that can?" implicitly asks readers to recall an important distinction just made (the definitions of offshorable and non-offshorable jobs) and then clearly moves readers forward to new, related content. As you can see, the openings of paragraphs 5 and 10 announce new sections in the article.

Each section of an article generally takes several paragraphs to develop. Between paragraphs, and almost certainly between sections of an article, you will usually find transitions that help you understand what you have just read and what you are about to read. For articles that have no subheadings, try writing your own section headings in the margins as you take notes. Blinder's article can be divided into five sections.

Section 1: Recent past: education of workers important—For twenty-five years, the labor market has rewarded workers with higher levels of education (paragraphs 1–4).

Section 2: Future: ed level won't always matter—workers in service sector will lose jobs offshore—Once thought immune to outsourcing, even highly trained service workers will lose jobs to overseas competition (paragraphs 5–9).

Section 3: Which service jobs at highest risk? Personal service workers are safe; impersonal service workers, both highly educated and not, will see jobs offshored (paragraphs 10–15).

Section 4: Educating the future workforce—Emphasizing the kind, not amount, of education will help to prepare workers for jobs of the future (paragraphs 16–22).

Section 5: Needed policy reforms—Government can improve conditions for low-end service workers and expand opportunities for higher-end service workers; start with education (paragraphs 23–26).

Write a Brief Summary of Each Stage of Thought

The purpose of this step is to wean yourself from the language of the original passage, so that you are not tied to it when writing the summary. Here are brief summaries, one for each stage of thought in "Will Your Job Be Exported?"

Section 1: Recent past: education of workers important (paragraphs 1–4).

For the past twenty-five years, the greater a worker's skill or level of education, the better and more stable the job.

Section 2: Future: ed level won't always matter—workers in service sector will lose jobs offshore (paragraphs 5–9).

Advances in technology have brought to the service sector the same pressures that forced so many manufacturing jobs offshore to China and India. The rate of offshoring in the service sector will accelerate and "eventually exceed" job losses in manufacturing, says Blinder, and jobs requiring both relatively little education (like call-center staffing) and extensive education (like software development) will be lost to workers overseas.

Section 3: Which service jobs at highest risk? (paragraphs 10–15).

While "personal services" workers (like barbers and surgeons) will be relatively safe from offshoring because their work requires close physical proximity to customers, "impersonal services" workers (like call-center operators and radiologists), regardless of their skill or education, will be at risk because their work can be completed remotely without loss of quality and then delivered via phone or computer. Blinder believes that "the relative demand for labor in the United States will [probably] shift away from impersonal services and toward personal services."

Section 4: Educating the future workforce (paragraphs 16–22).

Blinder advises young people to plan for "a high-end personal service occupation that is not offshorable." He also urges educators to prepare the future workforce by anticipating the needs of a personal services economy and redesigning classroom instruction and vocational training accordingly.

Section 5: Needed policy reforms (paragraphs 23–26).

Blinder urges the government to develop policies that will improve wages and conditions for low-wage personal service workers (like janitors); to encourage more low-wage workers

(like daycare providers) to retrain and take on better jobs; and
to increase opportunities for professional and vocational training in high-demand areas (like nursing and carpentry).

Write a Thesis: A Brief Summary of the Entire Passage

The thesis is the most general statement of a summary (or any
other type of academic writing). It is the statement that
announces the paper's subject and the claim that you or—in
the case of a summary—another author will be making about
that subject. Every paragraph of a paper illuminates the thesis
by providing supporting detail or explanation. The relationship of these paragraphs to the thesis is analogous to the
relationship of the sentences within a paragraph to the topic
sentence. Both the thesis and the topic sentences are general
statements (the thesis being the more general) that are followed by systematically arranged details.

To ensure clarity for the reader, *the first sentence of your
summary should begin with the author's thesis, regardless of where it
appears in the article itself.* An author may locate her thesis at the
beginning of her work, in which case the thesis operates as a
general principle from which details of the presentation
follow. This is called a *deductive* organization: thesis first,
supporting details second. Alternatively, an author may locate
his thesis at the end of the work, in which case the author
begins with specific details and builds toward a more general
conclusion, or thesis. This is called an *inductive* organization.
And, as you might expect, an author might locate the thesis
anywhere between beginning and end, at whatever point it
seems best positioned.*

---

*Blinder positions his thesis midway through his five-section article. He opens
the selection by discussing the role of education in the labor market during the
past twenty-five years (Section 1, pars. 1–4). He continues by summarizing an
earlier article on the ways in which service jobs are following manufacturing
jobs offshore (Section 2, pars. 5–9). He then presents a two-sentence thesis in
answer to the question that opens paragraph 10: "What distinguishes the jobs
that cannot be offshored from the ones that can?" The remainder of the article
either develops this thesis (Section 3, pars. 10–15) or follows its implications for
education (Section 4, pars. 16–22) and public policy (Section 5, pars. 23–26).

A thesis consists of a subject and an assertion about that subject. How can we go about fashioning an adequate thesis for a summary of Blinder's article? Probably no two versions of Blinder's thesis statement would be worded identically, but it is fair to say that any reasonable thesis will indicate that Blinder's subject is the future loss to offshoring of American jobs in the service sector—that part of the economy that delivers services to consumers, from low end (e.g., janitorial services) to high end (e.g., neurosurgery). How does Blinder view the situation? How secure will service jobs be if Blinder's distinction between personal and impersonal services is valid? Looking back over our section summaries, we find that Blinder insists on three points: (1) that education and skill matter less than they once did in determining job quality and security; (2) that the distinction between personal and impersonal services will increasingly determine which jobs remain and which are offshored; and (3) that the distinction between personal and impersonal has implications for the future of both education and public policy.

Does Blinder make a statement anywhere in this passage that pulls all this together? Examine paragraph 10 and you will find his thesis—two sentences that answer his question about which jobs will and will not be sent offshore: "The crucial distinction is not—and this is the central point of this essay—the required levels of skill and education. ...Instead, the new critical distinction may be that some services either require personal delivery (e.g., driving a taxi and brain surgery) or are seriously degraded when delivered electronically (e.g., college teaching—at least, I hope!), while other jobs (e.g., call centers and keyboard data entry) are not."

You may have learned that a thesis statement must be expressed in a single sentence. We would offer a slight rewording of this generally sound advice and say that a thesis statement must be *expressible* in a single sentence. For reasons of emphasis or style, a writer might choose to distribute a thesis across two or more sentences. Certainly, the sense of Blinder's thesis can take the form of a single statement: "The critical distinction is X, not Y." For reasons largely of emphasis, he divides his thesis into two sentences—in fact, separating these sentences with another sentence that explains the first part of the thesis: "These attributes [that is, skill and education] have been critical to labor-market success in the past, but may be less so in the future."

Here is a one-sentence version of Blinder's two-sentence thesis:

> The quality and security of future jobs in America's service sector will be determined by how "offshorable" those jobs are.

Notice that the statement anticipates a summary of the *entire* article: both the discussion leading up to Blinder's thesis and his discussion after. To clarify for our readers the fact that this idea is Blinder's and not ours, we might qualify the thesis as follows:

> In "Will Your Job Be Exported?" economist Alan S. Blinder argues that the quality and security of future jobs in America's service sector will be determined by how "offshorable" those jobs are.

The first sentence of a summary is crucially important, for it orients readers by letting them know what to expect in the coming paragraphs. In the example above, the sentence refers directly to an article, its author, and the thesis for the upcoming summary. The author and title reference could also be indicated in the summary's title (if this were a freestanding summary), in which case their mention could be dropped from the thesis statement. And lest you become frustrated too quickly with how much effort it takes to come up with this crucial sentence, keep in mind that writing an acceptable thesis for a summary takes time. In this case, it took three drafts, roughly ten minutes, to compose a thesis and another few minutes of fine-tuning after a draft of the entire summary was completed. The thesis needed revision because the first draft was vague; the second draft was improved but too specific on a secondary point; the third draft was more complete but too general on a key point:

> *Draft 1:* We must begin now to train young people for high-quality personal service jobs.

(Vague. The question of why we should begin training isn't clear, nor is the phrase "high-quality personal service jobs." Define this term or make it more general.)

Draft 2: Alan S. Blinder argues that unlike in the past, the quality and security of future American jobs will not be determined by skill level or education but rather by how "offshorable" those jobs are. (Better, but the reference to "skill level or education" is secondary to Blinder's main point about offshorable jobs.)

Draft 3: In "Will Your Job Be Exported?" economist Alan S. Blinder argues that the quality and security of future jobs will be determined by how "offshorable" those jobs are. (Close—but not "all" jobs. Blinder specifies which types of jobs are "offshorable.")

Final Draft: In "Will Your Job Be Exported?" economist Alan S. Blinder argues that the quality and security of future jobs in America's service sector will be determined by how "offshorable" those jobs are.

Write the First Draft of the Summary

Let's consider two possible summaries of Blinder's article: (1) a short summary, combining a thesis with brief section summaries, and (2) a longer summary, combining thesis, brief section summaries, and some carefully chosen details. Again, keep in mind that you are reading final versions; each of the following summaries is the result of at least two full drafts. Highlighting indicates transitions added to smooth the flow of the summary.

Summary 1: Combine Thesis Sentence with Brief Section Summaries

1   In "Will Your Job Be Exported?" economist Alan S. Blinder argues that the quality and security of future jobs in America's service sector will be determined by how "offshorable" those jobs are. For the past twenty-five years, the greater a worker's skill or level of education, the better and more stable the job. No longer. Advances in technology have brought to the service sector the same

pressures that forced so many manufacturing jobs offshore to China and India. The rate of offshoring in the
service sector will accelerate, and jobs requiring both
relatively little education (like call-center staffing) and
extensive education (like software development) will
increasingly be lost to workers overseas.

2   These losses will "eventually exceed" losses in manufacturing, but not all services jobs are equally at risk.
While "personal services" workers (like barbers and
surgeons) will be relatively safe from offshoring because
their work requires close physical proximity to customers, "impersonal services" workers (like call-center
operators and radiologists), regardless of their skill or
education, will be at risk because their work can be completed remotely without loss of quality and then delivered via phone or computer. "[T]he relative demand
for labor in the United States will [probably] shift away
from impersonal services and toward personal services."

3   Blinder recommends three courses of action: He
advises young people to plan for "a high-end personal
service occupation that is not offshorable." He urges
educators to prepare the future workforce by anticipating the needs of a personal services economy and
redesigning classroom instruction and vocational
training accordingly. Finally, he urges the government to adopt policies that will improve existing personal services jobs by increasing wages for low-wage
workers; retraining workers to take on better jobs;
and increasing opportunities in high-demand, well-
paid areas like nursing and carpentry. Ultimately,
Blinder wants America to prepare a new generation to
"lead and innovate" in an economy that will continue
exporting jobs that require "following and copying."

The Strategy of the Shorter Summary

This short summary consists essentially of a restatement of
Blinder's thesis plus the section summaries, modified or

expanded a little for stylistic purposes. You'll recall that Blinder locates his thesis midway through the article, in paragraph 10. But note that this model summary *begins* with a restatement of his thesis. Notice also the relative weight given to the section summaries within the model. Blinder's main point, his "critical distinction" between personal and impersonal services jobs, is summarized in paragraph 2 of the model. The other paragraphs combine summaries of relatively less important (that is, supporting or explanatory) material. Paragraph 1 combines summaries of the article's Sections 1 and 2; paragraph 3 combines summaries of Sections 4 and 5.

Between the thesis and the section summaries, notice the insertion of three (highlighted) transitions. The first—a fragment (*No longer*)—bridges the first paragraph's summaries of Sections 1 and 2 of Blinder's article. The second transition links a point Blinder makes in his Section 2 (*Losses in the service sector will "eventually exceed" losses in manufacturing*) with an introduction to the key point he will make in Section 3 (*Not all service jobs are equally at risk*). The third transition (*Blinder recommends three courses of action*) bridges the summary of Blinder's Section 3 to summaries of Sections 4 and 5. Each transition, then, links sections of the whole: each casts the reader back to recall points just made; each casts the reader forward by announcing related points about to be made. Our model ends with a summary of Blinder's motivation for writing, the sense of which is implied by the section summaries but nowhere made explicit.

Summary 2: Combine Thesis Sentence, Section Summaries, and Carefully Chosen Details

The thesis and brief section summaries could also be used as the outline for a more detailed summary. However, most of the details in the passage won't be necessary in a summary. It isn't necessary even in a longer summary of this passage to discuss all of Blinder's examples of jobs that are more or less likely to be sent offshore. It would be appropriate, though, to mention one example of such a job; to review his reasons for thinking "that service-sector offshoring will eventually exceed manufacturing-sector offshoring by a hefty margin"; and to expand on his point that a college education in itself will no longer ensure job security.

None of these details appeared in the first summary; but in a longer summary, a few carefully selected details might be desirable for clarity. How do you decide which details to include? First, working with Blinder's point that one's job type (personal services vs. impersonal services) will matter more for future job quality and security than did the once highly regarded "silver bullet" of education, you may want to cite some of the most persuasive evidence supporting this idea. For example, you could explore why some highly paid physicians, like radiologists, might find themselves competing for jobs with lower-paid physicians overseas. Further, your expanded summary might reflect the relative weight Blinder gives to education (seven paragraphs, the longest of the article's five sections).

You won't always know which details to include and which to exclude. Developing good judgment in comprehending and summarizing texts is largely a matter of reading skill and prior knowledge (see "Using the Summary"). Consider the analogy of the seasoned mechanic who can pinpoint an engine problem by simply listening to a characteristic sound that to a less-experienced person is just noise. Or consider the chess player who can plot three separate winning strategies from a board position that to a novice looks like a hopeless jumble. In the same way, the more practiced a reader you are, the more knowledgeable you will become about the subject and the better able you will be to make critical distinctions between elements of greater and lesser importance. In the meantime, read as carefully as you can and use your own best judgment as to how to present your material.

Here's one version of a completed summary with carefully chosen details. Note that we have highlighted phrases and sentences added to the original, briefer summary.

1   In "Will Your Job Be Exported?" economist Alan S.
    Blinder argues that the quality and security of future
    jobs in America's service sector will be determined
    by how "offshorable" those jobs are. For the past
    twenty-five years, the greater a worker's skill or
    level of education, the better and more stable the job.

Americans have long regarded education as the "silver bullet" that could propel motivated people to better jobs and a better life. No longer. Advances in technology have brought to the service sector the same pressures that forced so many manufacturing jobs offshore to China and India. The rate of offshoring in the service sector will accelerate, says Blinder, and jobs requiring both relatively little education (like call-center staffing) and extensive education (like software development) will increasingly be lost to workers overseas.

2   Blinder expects that job losses in the service sector will "eventually exceed" losses in manufacturing, for three reasons. Developed countries have more service jobs than manufacturing jobs; as technology speeds communications, more service jobs will be offshorable; and the numbers of qualified offshore workers is increasing. Service jobs lost to foreign competition may cause a "bumpy" period as the global economy sorts out what work gets done where, by whom. In time, as the global economy finds its "eventual equilibrium," offshoring will benefit the United States; but the consequences in the meantime may be painful for many.

3   That pain will not be shared equally by all service workers, however. While "personal service" workers (like barbers and surgeons) will be relatively safe from offshoring because their work requires close physical proximity to customers, "impersonal service" workers (like audio transcribers and radiologists), regardless of their skill or education, will be at risk because their work can be completed remotely without loss of quality and then delivered via phone or computer. In the coming decades, says Blinder, "the relative demand for labor in the United States will [probably] shift away from impersonal services and toward personal services." This shift will be influenced by the desire to keep good jobs in the United States while exporting

jobs that require "following and copying." Highly trained computer coders will face the same pressures of outsourcing as relatively untrained call-center attendants. A tax attorney whose work requires no face-to-face interaction with clients may see her work migrate overseas while a divorce attorney, who must interact with clients on a case-by-case basis, may face no such competition. Same educations, different outcomes: what determines their fates in a global economy is the nature of their work (that is, personal vs. impersonal), not their level of education.

4   Based on this analysis, Blinder recommends three courses of action: First, he advises young people to plan for "a high-end personal service occupation that is not offshorable." Many good jobs, like carpentry and plumbing, will not require a college degree. Next, Blinder urges educators to prepare the future workforce by anticipating the needs of a personal services economy and redesigning classroom instruction and vocational training accordingly. These efforts should begin in elementary school and develop imagination and interpersonal skills rather than capacities for rote memorization. Finally, Blinder urges the government to develop policies that will improve wages and conditions for low-wage personal services workers (like janitors); to encourage more low-wage workers (like daycare providers) to retrain and take on better service jobs; and to increase opportunities for professional and vocational training for workers in high-demand services areas (like nurses and electricians). Ultimately, Blinder wants America to prepare a new generation of workers who will "lead and innovate...just as we have in the past."

The Strategy of the Longer Summary

Compared to the first, briefer summary, this effort (seventy percent longer than the first) includes Blinder's reasons for suggesting that job losses in the services sector will exceed losses in manufacturing. It emphasizes Blinder's point that job type (personal vs. impersonal services), not a worker's education level, will ensure job security. It includes Blinder's point that offshoring in the service sector is part of a larger global economy seeking "equilibrium." And it offers more on Blinder's thoughts concerning the education of future workers.

The final two of our suggested steps for writing summaries are (1) to check your summary against the original passage, making sure that you have included all the important ideas, and (2) to revise so that the summary reads smoothly and coherently. The structure of this summary generally reflects the structure of the original article—with one significant departure, as noted earlier. Blinder uses a modified inductive approach, stating his thesis midway through the article. The summary, however, states the thesis immediately, then proceeds deductively to develop that thesis.

HOW LONG SHOULD A SUMMARY BE?

The length of a summary depends both on the length of the original passage and on the use to which the summary will be put. If you are summarizing an entire article, a good rule of thumb is that your summary should be no longer than one-fourth the length of the original passage. Of course, if you were summarizing an entire chapter or even an entire book, it would have to be much shorter than that. The longer summary above is one-quarter the length of Alan Blinder's original. Although it shouldn't be very much longer, you have seen (see Summary 1 under "Write the First Draft of the Summary") that it could be quite a bit shorter.

The length as well as the content of the summary also depends on the *purpose* to which it will be put. Let's suppose you decided to use Blinder's piece in a paper that deals with the loss of manufacturing jobs in the United States and the rise of the service economy. In this case, in an effort to explain the complexities of the service economy to your readers, you might summarize *only* Blinder's core distinction between jobs in personal services and impersonal services, likely mentioning that jobs in the latter category are at risk of offshoring. If, instead, you were writing a paper in which you argued that the forces of globalization will eventually collapse the world's economies into a single, global economy, you would likely give less attention to Blinder's distinction between personal and impersonal services. More to the point might be his observation that highly skilled, highly educated workers in the United States are now finding themselves competing with qualified, lower-wage workers in China and India. Thus, depending on your purpose, you would summarize either selected portions of a source or an entire source. We will see this process more fully demonstrated in the upcoming chapters on syntheses.

AVOIDING PLAGIARISM

Plagiarism is generally defined as the attempt to pass off the work of another as one's own. Whether born out of calculation or desperation, plagiarism is the least tolerated offense in the academic world. The fact that most plagiarism is unintentional—arising from an ignorance of the conventions rather than deceitfulness—makes no difference to many professors.

The ease of cutting and pasting whole blocks of text from Web sources into one's own paper makes it tempting for some to take the easy way out and avoid doing their own research and writing. But, apart from the serious ethical issues involved, the same technology that makes such acts possible also makes it possible for instructors to detect them. Software marketed to instructors allows them to conduct Web searches, using suspicious phrases as keywords. The results often provide irrefutable evidence of plagiarism.

Of course, plagiarism is not confined to students. Recent years have seen a number of high-profile cases—some of them reaching the front pages of newspapers—of well-known scholars who were shown to have copied passages from sources into their own book manuscripts, without proper attribution. In some cases, the scholars maintained that these appropriations were simply a matter of carelessness, that in the press and volume of work, they had lost track of which words were theirs and which were the words of their sources. But such excuses sounded hollow: These careless acts inevitably embarrassed the scholars professionally, tarnished their otherwise fine work and reputations, and disappointed their many admirers.

You can avoid plagiarism and charges of plagiarism by following the basic rules provided in the box at the end of the chapter.

Following is a passage from an article by Richard Rovere on Senator Joseph P. McCarthy, along with several student versions of the ideas represented.

> McCarthy never seemed to believe in himself or in anything he had said. He knew that Communists were not in charge of American foreign policy. He knew that they weren't running the United States Army. He knew that he had spent five years looking for Communists in the government and that—although some must certainly have been there, since Communists had turned up in practically every other major government in the world—he hadn't come up with even one.

One student version of this passage reads:

> McCarthy never believed in himself or in anything he had said. He knew that Communists were not in charge of American foreign policy and weren't running the United States Army. He knew that he had spent five years looking for Communists in the government, and although there must certainly have been some there, since Communists were in practically every other major government in the world, he hadn't come up with even one.

Clearly, this is intentional plagiarism. The student has copied the original passage almost word for word.

Here is another version of the same passage:

> McCarthy knew that Communists were not running foreign policy or the Army. He also knew that although there must have been some Communists in the government, he hadn't found a single one, even though he had spent five years looking.

This student has attempted to put the ideas into her own words, but both the wording and the sentence structure are so heavily dependent on the original passage that even if it *were* cited, most professors would consider it plagiarism.

In the following version, the student has sufficiently changed the wording and sentence structure, and she uses a *signal phrase* (a phrase used to introduce a quotation or paraphrase, signaling to the reader that the words to follow come from someone else) to properly credit the information to Rovere, so that there is no question of plagiarism:

> According to Richard Rovere, McCarthy was fully aware that Communists were running neither the government nor the Army. He also knew that he hadn't found a single Communist in government, even after a lengthy search (192).

And although this is not a matter of plagiarism, it's essential to quote accurately. You are not permitted to change any part of a quotation or to omit any part of it without using brackets or ellipses.

RULES FOR AVOIDING PLAGIARISM

- Cite *all* quoted material and *all* summarized and paraphrased material, unless the information is common knowledge (e.g., the Civil War was fought from 1861 to 1865).
- Make sure that both the *wording* and the *sentence structure* of your summaries and paraphrases are substantially your own.

2
Critical Reading and Critique

CRITICAL READING

When writing papers in college, you are often called on to respond critically to source materials. Critical reading requires the abilities to both summarize and evaluate a presentation. As you have seen in Chapter 1, a *summary* is a brief restatement in your own words of the content of a passage. An *evaluation* is a more ambitious undertaking. In your college work, you read to gain and *use* new information. But because sources are not equally valid or equally useful, you must learn to distinguish critically among them by evaluating them.

There is no ready-made formula for determining validity. Critical reading and its written equivalent—the *critique*— require discernment, sensitivity, imagination, knowledge of the subject, and above all, willingness to become involved in what you read. These skills are developed only through repeated practice. But you must begin somewhere, and so we recommend you start by posing two broad questions about passages, articles, and books that you read: (1) To what extent does the author succeed in his or her purpose? (2) To what extent do you agree with the author?

Question 1: To What Extent Does the Author Succeed in His or Her Purpose?

All critical reading *begins with an accurate summary*. Before attempting an evaluation, you must be able to locate an author's thesis and identify the selection's content and structure. You must understand the author's *purpose*. Authors write to inform, to persuade, and to entertain. A given piece may be primarily *informative* (a summary of the research on cloning), primarily *persuasive* (an argument on what the government should do to alleviate homelessness), or primarily *entertaining* (a play about the frustrations of young lovers). Or it may be all three (as in John Steinbeck's novel *The Grapes of Wrath,* about migrant workers during the Great Depression). Sometimes authors are not fully conscious of their purpose. Sometimes their purpose changes as they write. Also, multiple purposes can overlap: A piece of writing may need to inform the reader about an issue in order to make a persuasive point. But if the finished piece is coherent, it will have a primary reason for having been written, and it should be apparent that the author is attempting primarily to inform, persuade, or entertain a particular audience. To identify this primary reason—this purpose—is your first job as a critical reader. Your next job is to determine how successful the author has been in achieving this objective.

As a critical reader, you bring various criteria, or standards of judgment, to bear when you read pieces intended to inform, persuade, or entertain.

Writing to Inform

A piece intended to inform will provide definitions, describe or report on a process, recount a story, give historical background, and/or provide facts and figures. An informational piece responds to questions such as:

What (or who) is _____?

How does _____ work?

What is the controversy or problem about?

What happened?

How and why did it happen?

What were the results?

What are the arguments for and against _____?

WHERE DO WE FIND WRITTEN CRITIQUES?

Here are just a few of the types of writing that involve critique:

Academic Writing

- **Research papers** critique sources in order to establish their usefulness.
- **Position papers** stake out a position by critiquing other positions.
- **Book reviews** combine summary with critique.
- **Essay exams** demonstrate understanding of course material by critiquing it.

Workplace Writing

- **Legal briefs and legal arguments** critique previous arguments made or anticipated by opposing counsel.
- **Business plans and proposals** critique other less cost-effective, efficient, or reasonable approaches.
- **Policy briefs** communicate strengths and weaknesses of policies and legislation through critique.

To the extent that an author answers these and related questions and that the answers are a matter of verifiable record (you could check for accuracy if you had the time and inclination), the selection is intended to inform. Having identified such an intention, you can organize your response by considering three other criteria: accuracy, significance, and fair interpretation of information.

Evaluating Informative Writing

Accuracy of Information. If you are going to use any of the information presented, you must be satisfied that it is trustworthy. One of your responsibilities as a critical reader, then, is to find out if the information is accurate. This means you should check facts against other sources. Government publications are often good resources for verifying facts about political legislation, population data, crime statistics, and the like. You can also search key terms in library databases and on the Web. Since material on the Web is essentially self-published, however, you must be especially vigilant in assessing its legitimacy. A wealth of useful information is now available on the Internet—as are distorted "facts," unsupported opinion, and hidden agendas.

Significance of Information. One useful question that you can put to a reading is "So what?" In the case of selections that attempt to inform, you may reasonably wonder whether the information makes a difference. What can the reader gain from this information? How is knowledge advanced by the publication of this material? Is the information of importance to you or to others in a particular audience? Why or why not?

Fair Interpretation of Information. At times you will read reports whose sole purpose is to relate raw data or information. In these cases, you will build your response on Question 1, introduced earlier: To what extent does the author succeed in his or her purpose? More frequently, once an author has presented information, he or she will attempt to evaluate or interpret it—which is only reasonable, since information that has not been evaluated or interpreted is of little use. One of your tasks as a critical reader is to make a distinction between the author's presentation of facts and figures and his or her attempts to evaluate them. Watch for shifts from straightforward descriptions of factual information ("20 percent of the population") to assertions about what this information means ("a *mere* 20 percent of the population"), what its implications are, and so on. Pay attention to whether the logic with which the author connects interpretation with facts is sound. You may find that the information is valuable but the interpretation is not. Perhaps the author's conclusions are not justified. Could you offer a contrary explanation for the same facts? Does more information need to be gathered before firm conclusions can be drawn? Why?

Writing to Persuade

Writing is frequently intended to persuade—that is, to influence the reader's thinking. To make a persuasive case, the writer must begin with an assertion that is arguable, some statement about which reasonable people could disagree. Such an assertion, when it serves as the essential organizing principle of the article or book, is called a *thesis*. Here are two examples:

> Because they do not speak English, many children in this affluent land are being denied their fundamental right to equal educational opportunity.

> Bilingual education, which has been stridently promoted by a small group of activists with their own agenda, is detrimental to the very students it is supposed to serve.

Thesis statements such as these—and the subsequent assertions used to help support them—represent conclusions that authors have drawn as a result of researching and thinking about an issue. You go through the same process yourself when you write persuasive papers or critiques. And just as you are entitled to evaluate critically the assertions of authors you read, so your professors—and other students—are entitled to evaluate *your* assertions, whether they be written arguments or comments made in class discussion.

Keep in mind that writers organize arguments by arranging evidence to support one conclusion and to oppose (or dismiss) another. You can assess the validity of an argument and its conclusion by determining whether the author has (1) clearly defined key terms, (2) used information fairly, and (3) argued logically and not fallaciously (see section on "Logical Argumentation: Avoiding Logical Fallacies" below).

Evaluating Persuasive Writing

Read the argument that follows on the cancellation of the National Aeronautics and Space Administration's lunar program. We will illustrate our discussion on defining terms, using information fairly, and arguing logically by referring to

Charles Krauthammer's argument, which appeared as an op-ed in the *Washington Post* on July 17, 2009. The model critique that follows these illustrations will be based on this same argument.

The Moon We Left Behind

Charles Krauthammer

1   Michael Crichton once wrote that if you told a physicist in 1899 that within a hundred years humankind would, among other wonders (nukes, commercial airlines), "travel to the moon, and then lose interest . . . the physicist would almost certainly pronounce you mad." In 2000, I quoted these lines expressing Crichton's incredulity at America's abandonment of the moon. It is now 2009 and the moon recedes ever further.

2   Next week marks the 40th anniversary of the first moon landing. We say we will return in 2020. But that promise was made by a previous president, and this president [Obama] has defined himself as the antimatter to George Bush. Moreover, for all of Barack Obama's Kennedyesque qualities, he has expressed none of Kennedy's enthusiasm for human space exploration.

3   So with the Apollo moon program long gone, and with Constellation,* its supposed successor, still little more than a hope, we remain in retreat from space. Astonishing. After countless millennia of gazing and dreaming, we finally got off the ground at Kitty Hawk in 1903. Within 66 years, a nanosecond in human history, we'd landed on the moon. Then five more landings, 10 more moonwalkers and, in the decades since, nothing.

4   To be more precise: almost 40 years spent in low Earth orbit studying, well, zero-G nausea and sundry cosmic mysteries. We've done it with the most beautiful, intricate, complicated—and ultimately, hopelessly impractical—machine ever built by

---

*Constellation was a NASA human spaceflight program designed to develop post space shuttle vehicles capable of traveling to the moon and perhaps to Mars. Authorized in 2005, the program was canceled by President Obama in 2010.

man: the space shuttle. We turned this magnificent bird into a truck for hauling goods and people to a tinkertoy we call the international space station, itself created in a fit of post-Cold War internationalist absentmindedness as a place where people of differing nationality can sing "Kumbaya" while weightless.

5   The shuttle is now too dangerous, too fragile and too expensive. Seven more flights and then it is retired, going—like the Spruce Goose** and the Concorde†—into the Museum of Things Too Beautiful and Complicated to Survive.

6   America's manned space program is in shambles. Fourteen months from today, for the first time since 1962, the United States will be incapable not just of sending a man to the moon but of sending anyone into Earth orbit. We'll be totally grounded. We'll have to beg a ride from the Russians or perhaps even the Chinese.

7   So what, you say? Don't we have problems here on Earth? Oh, please. Poverty and disease and social ills will always be with us. If we'd waited for them to be rectified before venturing out, we'd still be living in caves.

8   Yes, we have a financial crisis. No one's asking for a crash Manhattan Project. All we need is sufficient funding from the hundreds of billions being showered from Washington—"stimulus" monies that, unlike Eisenhower's interstate highway system or Kennedy's Apollo program, will leave behind not a trace on our country or our consciousness—to build Constellation and get us back to Earth orbit and the moon a half-century after the original landing.

**Spruce Goose was the informal name bestowed by critics on the H4 Hercules, a heavy transport aircraft designed and built during World War II by the Hughes Aircraft Company. Built almost entirely of birch (not spruce) because of wartime restrictions on war materials, the aircraft boasted the largest height and wingspan of any aircraft in history. Only one prototype was built, and the aircraft made only one flight, on November 2, 1947. It is currently housed at the Evergreen Aviation Museum in McMinnville, Oregon.

†Admired for its elegant design as well as its speed, the Concorde was a supersonic passenger airliner built by a British-French consortium. It was first flown in 1969, entered service in 1976 (with regular flights to and from London, Paris, Washington, and New York), and was retired in 2003, a casualty of economic pressures. Only twenty Concordes were built.

9   Why do it? It's not for practicality. We didn't go to the moon to spin off cooling suits and freeze-dried fruit. Any technological return is a bonus, not a reason. We go for the wonder and glory of it. Or, to put it less grandly, for its immense possibilities. We choose to do such things, said JFK, "not because they are easy, but because they are hard." And when you do such magnificently hard things—send sailing a Ferdinand Magellan or a Neil Armstrong—you open new human possibility in ways utterly unpredictable.

10   The greatest example? Who could have predicted that the moon voyages would create the most potent impetus to—and symbol of—environmental consciousness here on Earth: Earthrise, the now iconic Blue Planet photograph brought back by Apollo 8?

11   Ironically, that new consciousness about the uniqueness and fragility of Earth focused contemporary imagination away from space and back to Earth. We are now deep into that hyper-terrestrial phase, the age of iPod and *Facebook*, of social networking and eco-consciousness.

12   But look up from your BlackBerry one night. That is the moon. On it are exactly 12 sets of human footprints—untouched, unchanged, abandoned. For the first time in history, the moon is not just a mystery and a muse, but a nightly rebuke. A vigorous young president once summoned us to this new frontier, calling the voyage "the most hazardous and dangerous and greatest adventure on which man has ever embarked." And so we did it. We came. We saw. Then we retreated.

13   How could we?

Persuasive Strategies

Clearly Defined Terms. The validity of an argument depends to some degree on how carefully an author has defined key terms. Take the assertion, for example, that American society must be grounded in "family values." Just what do people who use this phrase mean by it? The validity of their argument depends on whether they and their readers agree on a definition of "family values"—as well as what it means to be "grounded in" family values. If an author writes that in the recent past, "America's elites accepted as a matter of course that a free society can sustain itself only through virtue and temperance in the people," readers need to know what exactly the author means by "elites" and by "virtue and temperance" before they can assess the validity of the argument. In such cases, the success of the argument—its ability to persuade—hinges on the definition of a term. So, in responding to an argument, be sure you (and the author) are clear on what exactly is being argued. Unless you are, no informed response is possible.

Note that in addition to their *denotative* meaning (their specific or literal meaning), many words carry a *connotative* meaning (their suggestive, associative, or emotional meaning). For example, the denotative meaning of "home" is simply the house or apartment where one lives. But the connotative meaning—with its associations of family, belongingness, refuge, safety, and familiarity—adds a significant emotional component to this literal meaning. (See more on connotation in "Emotionally Loaded Terms" later in this chapter.)

In the course of his argument, Krauthammer writes of "America's abandonment of the moon" and of the fact that we have "retreated" from lunar exploration. Consider the words "abandon" and "retreat." What do these words mean to you? Look them up in a dictionary for precise definitions (note all possible meanings provided). In what contexts are we most likely to see these words used? What emotional meaning and significance do they generally carry? For example, what do we usually think of people who abandon a marriage or military units that retreat? To what extent does it appear to you that Krauthammer is using these words in accordance with one or more of their dictionary definitions, their denotations? To what extent does the force of his argument also depend upon the power of these words' connotative meanings?

When writing a paper, you will need to decide, like Krauthammer, which terms to define and which you can assume the reader will define in the same way you do. As the writer of a critique, you should identify and discuss any undefined or ambiguous term that might give rise to confusion.

Fair Use of Information. Information is used as evidence in support of arguments. When you encounter such evidence, ask yourself two questions: (1) "Is the information accurate and up to date?" At least a portion of an argument becomes invalid when the information used to support it is wrong or stale. (2) "Has the author cited *representative* information?" The evidence used in an argument must be presented in a spirit of fair play. An author is less than ethical when he presents only the evidence favoring his own views even though he is well aware that contrary evidence exists. For instance, it would be dishonest to argue that an economic recession is imminent and to cite only indicators of economic downturn while ignoring and failing to cite contrary (positive) evidence.

"The Moon We Left Behind" is not an information-heavy essay. The success of the piece turns on the author's powers of persuasion, not on his use of facts and figures. Krauthammer does, however, offer some key facts relating to Project Apollo and the fact that President Obama was not inclined to back a NASA-operated lunar-landing program. And, in fact, Krauthammer's fears were confirmed in February 2010, about six months after he wrote "The Moon We Left Behind," when the president canceled NASA's plans for further manned space exploration flights in favor of government support for commercial space operations.

Logical Argumentation: Avoiding Logical Fallacies

At some point, you'll need to respond to the logic of the argument itself. To be convincing, an argument should be governed by principles of *logic*—clear and orderly thinking. This does *not* mean that an argument cannot be biased. A biased argument—that is, an argument weighted toward one point of view and against others, which is in fact the nature of argument—may be valid as long as it is logically sound.

Let's examine several types of faulty thinking and logical fallacies you will need to watch for.

Emotionally Loaded Terms. Writers sometimes attempt to sway readers by using emotionally charged words. Words with positive connotations (e.g., "family values") are intended to sway readers to the author's point of view; words with negative connotations (e.g., "paying the price") try to sway readers away from an opposing point of view. The fact that an author uses emotionally loaded terms does not necessarily invalidate an argument. Emotional appeals are perfectly legitimate and time-honored modes of persuasion. But in academic writing, which is grounded in logical argumentation, they should not be the *only* means of persuasion. You should be sensitive to *how* emotionally loaded terms are being used. In particular, are they being used deceptively or to hide the essential facts?

We've already noted Krauthammer's use of the emotionally loaded terms "abandonment" and "retreat" when referring to the end of the manned space program. Notice also his use of the term "Kumbaya" in the sentence declaring that the international space station was "created in a fit of post-Cold War internationalist absentmindedness as a place where people of differing nationality can sing 'Kumbaya' while weightless." "Kumbaya" is an African-American spiritual dating from the 1930s, often sung by scouts around campfires. Jeffrey Weiss reports on the dual connotations of this word: "The song was originally associated with human and spiritual unity, closeness and compassion, and it still is, but more recently it is also cited or alluded to in satirical, sarcastic or even cynical ways that suggest blind or false moralizing, hypocrisy, or naively optimistic views of the world and human nature." Is Krauthammer drawing upon the emotional power of the original meaning or upon the more recent significance of this term? How does his particular use of "Kumbaya" strengthen (or weaken) his argument? What appears to be the difference in his mind between the value of the international space station and the value of returning to the moon? As someone evaluating the essay, you should be alert to this appeal to your emotions and then judge whether or not the appeal is fair and convincing. Above all, you should not let an emotional appeal blind you to shortcomings of logic, ambiguously defined terms, or a misuse of facts.

***Ad Hominem* Argument.** In an *ad hominem* argument, the writer rejects opposing views by attacking the person who holds them. By calling opponents names, an author avoids the issue. Consider this excerpt from a political speech:

> I could more easily accept my opponent's plan to increase revenues by collecting on delinquent tax bills if he had paid more than a hundred dollars in state taxes in each of the past three years. But the fact is, he's a millionaire with a millionaire's tax shelters. This man hasn't paid a wooden nickel for the state services he and his family depend on. So I ask you: Is *he* the one to be talking about taxes to *us*?

It could well be that the opponent has paid virtually no state taxes for three years; but this fact has nothing to do with, and is used as a ploy to divert attention from, the merits of a specific proposal for increasing revenues. The proposal is lost in the attack against the man himself, an attack that violates principles of logic. Writers (and speakers) should make their points by citing evidence in support of their views and by challenging contrary evidence.

In "The Moon We Left Behind," Krauthammer's only individual target is President Obama. While he does, at several points, unfavorably compare Obama to Kennedy, he does not do so in an *ad hominem* way. That is, he attacks Obama less for his personal qualities than for his policy decision to close down NASA's manned space program. At most, he laments that Obama "has expressed none of Kennedy's enthusiasm for human space exploration."

Faulty Cause and Effect. The fact that one event precedes another in time does not mean that the first event has caused the second. An example: Fish begin dying by the thousands in a lake near your hometown. An environmental group immediately cites chemical dumping by several manufacturing plants as the cause. But other causes are possible: A disease might have affected the fish; the growth of algae might have contributed to the deaths; or acid rain might be a factor. The origins of an event are usually complex and are not always traceable to a single cause. So you must carefully examine cause-and-effect reasoning when you find a writer using it. In Latin, this fallacy is known as *post hoc, ergo propter hoc* ("after this, therefore because of this").

Toward the end of "The Moon We Left Behind," Krauthammer declares that having turned our "imagination away from space and back to Earth . . . [w]e are now deep into that hyper-terrestrial phase, the age of iPod and *Facebook*, of social networking and eco-consciousness." He appears here to be suggesting a pattern of cause and effect: that as a people, we are no longer looking outward but, rather, turning inward; and this shift in our attention and focus has resulted in—or at least is a significant cause of—the death of the manned space program. Questions for a critique might include the following: (1) To what extent do you agree with Krauthammer's premise that we live in an inward-looking, rather than an outward-looking, age and that it is fair to call our present historical period "the age of iPod and Facebook"? (2) To what extent do you agree that because we may live in such an age, the space program no longer enjoys broad public or political support?

Either/Or Reasoning. Either/or reasoning also results from an unwillingness to recognize complexity. If in analyzing a problem an author artificially restricts the range of possible solutions by offering only two courses of action, and then rejects the one that he opposes, he cannot logically argue that the remaining course of action, which he favors, is therefore the only one that makes sense. Usually, several other options (at least) are possible. For whatever reason, the author has chosen to overlook them. As an example, suppose you are reading a selection on genetic engineering in which the author builds an argument on the basis of the following:

> Research in gene splicing is at a crossroads: Either scientists will be carefully monitored by civil authorities and their efforts limited

to acceptable applications, such as disease control; or, lacking regulatory guidelines, scientists will set their own ethical standards and begin programs in embryonic manipulation that, however well intended, exceed the proper limits of human knowledge.

Certainly, other possibilities for genetic engineering exist beyond the two mentioned here. But the author limits debate by establishing an either/or choice. Such a limitation is artificial and does not allow for complexity. As a critical reader, you need to be on the alert for reasoning based on restrictive, either/or alternatives.

TONE

Tone refers to the overall emotional effect produced by a writer's choice of language. Writers might use especially emphatic words to create a tone: A film reviewer might refer to a "magnificent performance," or a columnist might criticize "sleazeball politics."

These are extreme examples of tone; tone can also be more subtle, particularly if the writer makes a special effort *not* to inject emotion into the writing. As we indicated in the section on emotionally loaded terms, the fact that a writer's tone is highly emotional does not necessarily mean that the writer's argument is invalid. Conversely, a neutral tone does not ensure an argument's validity.

Many instructors discourage student writing that projects a highly emotional tone, considering it inappropriate for academic or preprofessional work. (One sure sign of emotion: the exclamation mark, which should be used sparingly.)

Hasty Generalization. Writers are guilty of hasty generalization when they draw their conclusions from too little evidence or from unrepresentative evidence. To argue that scientists should not proceed with the Human Genome Project because a recent editorial urged that the project be abandoned is to make a hasty generalization. That lone editorial may be unrepresentative of the views of most individuals—both scientists and laypeople—who have studied and written about the matter. To argue that one should never obey authority because Stanley Milgram's Yale University experiments in the 1960s showed the dangers of obedience is to ignore the fact that Milgram's experiments were concerned primarily with obedience to *immoral* authority. The experimental situation was unrepresentative of most routine demands for obedience—for example, to obey a parental rule or to comply with a summons for jury duty—and a conclusion about the malevolence of all authority would be a hasty generalization.

False Analogy. Comparing one person, event, or issue to another may be illuminating, but it can also be confusing or misleading. Differences between the two may be more significant than their similarities, and conclusions drawn from one may not necessarily apply to the other. A candidate for governor or president who argues that her experience as CEO of a major business would make her effective in governing a state or the country is assuming an analogy between the business and the political/civic worlds that does not hold up to examination. Most businesses are hierarchical, or top down: when a CEO issues an order, he or she can expect it to be carried out without argument. But governors and presidents command only their own executive branches. They cannot issue orders to independent legislatures or courts (much less private citizens); they can only attempt to persuade. In this case the implied analogy fails to convince the thoughtful reader or listener.

Begging the Question. To beg the question is to assume as proven fact the very thesis being argued. To assert, for example, that America does not need a new health care delivery system because America currently has the best health care in the world does not prove anything: It merely repeats the claim in different—and equally unproven—words. This fallacy is also known as *circular reasoning*.

Non Sequitur. *Non sequitur* is Latin for "it does not follow"; the term is used to describe a conclusion that does not logically follow from the premise. "Since minorities have made such great strides in the past few decades," a writer may argue, "we no longer need affirmative action programs." Aside from the fact that the premise itself is arguable (*have* minorities made such great strides?), it does not follow that because minorities *may* have made great strides, there is no further need for affirmative action programs.

Oversimplification. Be alert for writers who offer easy solutions to complicated problems. "America's economy will be strong again if we all 'buy American,'" a politician may argue. But the problems of America's economy are complex and cannot be solved by a slogan or a simple change in buying habits. Likewise, a writer who argues that we should ban genetic engineering assumes that simple solutions ("just say no") will be sufficient to deal with the complex moral dilemmas raised by this new technology.

Writing to Entertain

Authors write not only to inform and persuade but also to entertain. One response to entertainment is a hearty laugh, but it is possible to entertain without encouraging laughter: A good book or play or poem may prompt you to reflect, grow wistful, become elated, get angry. Laughter is only one of many possible reactions. Like a response to an informative piece or an argument, your response to an essay, poem, story, play, novel, or film should be precisely stated and carefully developed. Ask yourself some of the following questions (you won't have space to explore all of them, but try to consider the most important ones):

- Did I care for the portrayal of a certain character?
- Did that character (or a group of characters united by occupation, age, ethnicity, etc.) seem overly sentimental, for example, or heroic?
- Did his adversaries seem too villainous or stupid?
- Were the situations believable?
- Was the action interesting or merely formulaic?
- Was the theme developed subtly or powerfully, or did the work come across as preachy or unconvincing?

- Did the action at the end of the work follow plausibly from what had come before? Was the language fresh and incisive or stale and predictable?

Explain as specifically as possible what elements of the work seemed effective or ineffective and why. Offer an overall assessment, elaborating on your views.

Question 2: To What Extent Do You Agree with the Author?

A critical evaluation consists of two parts. The first part, just discussed, assesses the accuracy and effectiveness of an argument in terms of the author's logic and use of evidence. The second part, discussed here, responds to the argument—that is, agrees or disagrees with it.

Identify Points of Agreement and Disagreement

Be precise in identifying where you agree and disagree with an author. State as clearly as possible what *you* believe, in relation to what the author believes, as presented in the piece. Whether you agree enthusiastically, agree with reservations, or disagree, you can organize your reactions in two parts:

- Summarize the author's position.
- State your own position and explain why you believe as you do. The elaboration, in effect, becomes an argument itself, and this is true regardless of the position you take.

Any opinion that you express is effective to the extent you support it by supplying evidence from your reading (which should be properly cited), your observation, or your personal experience. Without such evidence, opinions cannot be authoritative. "I thought the article on inflation was lousy." Or: "It was terrific." Why? "I just thought so, that's all." Such opinions have no value because the criticism is imprecise: The critic has taken neither the time to read the article carefully nor the time to carefully explore his or her own reactions.

*Explore the Reasons for Agreement
and Disagreement: Evaluate Assumptions*

One way of elaborating your reactions to a reading is to explore the underlying *reasons* for agreement and disagreement. Your reactions are based largely on assumptions that you hold and how those assumptions compare with the author's. An *assumption* is a fundamental statement about the world and its operations that you take to be true. Often, a writer will express an assumption directly, as in this example:

> #1 One of government's most important functions is to raise and spend tax revenues on projects that improve the housing, medical, and nutritional needs of its citizens.

In this instance, the writer's claim is a direct expression of a fundamental belief about how the world, or some part of it, should work. The argumentative claim *is* the assumption. Just as often, an argument and its underlying assumption are not identical. In these cases, the assumption is some other statement that is implied by the argumentative claim—as in this example:

> #2 Human spaceflight is a waste of public money.

The logic of this second statement rests on an unstated assumption relating to the word *waste*. What, in this writer's view, is a *waste* of money? What is an effective or justified use? In order to agree or not with statement #2, a critical reader must know what assumption(s) it rests on. A good candidate for such an assumption would be statement #1. That is, a person who believes statement #1 about how governments ought to raise and spend money could well make statement #2. This may not be the only assumption underlying statement #2, but it could well be one of them.

Inferring and Implying Assumptions

Infer and *imply* are keywords relating to hidden, or unstated, assumptions; you should be clear on their meanings. A critical reader *infers* what is hidden in a statement and, through that inference, brings what is hidden into the open for examination.

Thus, the critical reader infers from statement #2 on human spaceflight the writer's assumption (statement #1) on how governments should spend money. At the same time, the writer of statement #2 *implies* (hints at but does not state directly) an assumption about how governments should spend money. There will be times when writers make statements and are unaware of their own assumptions.

Assumptions provide the foundation on which entire presentations are built. You may find an author's assumptions invalid—that is, not supported by factual evidence. You may disagree with value-based assumptions underlying an author's position—for instance, what constitutes "good" or "correct" behavior. In both cases, you may well disagree with the conclusions that follow from these assumptions. Alternatively, when you find that your own assumptions are contradicted by actual experience, you may be forced to conclude that certain of your fundamental beliefs about the world and how it works were mistaken.

An Example of Hidden Assumptions from the World of Finance

An interesting example of an assumption fatally colliding with reality was revealed during a recent congressional investigation into the financial meltdown of late 2008 precipitated by the collapse of the home mortgage market—itself precipitated, many believed, by an insufficiently regulated banking and financial system run amuck. During his testimony before the House Oversight Committee in October of that year, former Federal Reserve chairman Alan Greenspan was grilled by committee chairman Henry Waxman (D-CA) about his "ideology"—essentially an assumption or set of assumptions that become a governing principle. (In the following transcript, you can substitute the word "assumption" for "ideology.")

Greenspan responded, "I do have an ideology. My judgment is that free, competitive markets are by far the unrivaled way to organize economies. We have tried regulation; none meaningfully worked." Greenspan defined an ideology as "a conceptual framework [for] the way people deal with reality. Everyone has one. You have to. To exist, you need an ideology." And he pointed out that the assumptions on which he and the Federal Reserve operated were supported by "the best banking lawyers in the business . . . and an outside counsel of expert professionals to advise on regulatory matters."

Greenspan then admitted that in light of the economic disaster engulfing the nation, he had found a "flaw" in his ideology—that actual experience had violated some of his fundamental beliefs. The testimony continues:

> **Chairman Waxman:** You found a flaw?
>
> **Mr. Greenspan:** I found a flaw in the model that I perceived is the critical functioning structure that defines how the world works, so to speak.
>
> **Chairman Waxman:** In other words, you found that your view of the world, your ideology, was not right, it was not working.
>
> **Mr. Greenspan:** Precisely. That's precisely the reason I was shocked, because I had been going for 40 years or more with very considerable evidence that it was working exceptionally well.*

The lesson? All the research, expertise, and logical argumentation in the world will fail if the premise (assumption, ideology) on which it is based turns out to be "flawed."

How do you determine the validity of assumptions once you have identified them? In the absence of more scientific criteria, you start by considering how well the author's assumptions stack up against your own experience, observations, reading, and values—while remaining honestly aware of the limits of your own personal knowledge.

Readers will want to examine the assumption at the heart of Krauthammer's essay: that exploration and, particularly, the program to return human beings to the moon is a worthwhile enterprise. The writer of the critique that follows questions this assumption. But you may not: you may instead fully support

---

*United States. Cong. House Committee on Oversight and Government Reform. *The Financial Crisis and the Role of Federal Regulators.* 110th Cong., 2nd sess. Washington: GPO, 2008.

such a program. That's your decision, perhaps made even *before* you read Krauthammer's essay, perhaps as a *result* of having read it. What you must do as a critical reader is to recognize assumptions, whether they are stated or not. You should spell them out and then accept or reject them. Ultimately, your agreement or disagreement with an author will rest on your agreement or disagreement with that author's assumptions.

CRITIQUE

In Chapter 1 we focused on summary—the condensed presentation of ideas from another source. Summary is fundamental to much of academic writing because such writing relies so heavily on the works of others for the support of its claims. It's not going too far to say that summarizing is the critical thinking skill from which a majority of academic writing builds. However, most academic thinking and writing goes beyond summary. Generally, we use summary to restate our understanding of things we see or read. We then put that summary to use. In academic writing, one typical use of summary is as a prelude to critique.

A *critique* is a *formalized, critical reading of a passage*. It is also a personal response; but writing a critique is considerably more rigorous than saying that a movie is "great," or a book is "fascinating," or "I didn't like it." These are all responses, and, as such, they're a valid, even essential, part of your understanding of what you see and read. But such responses don't illuminate the subject—even for you—if you haven't explained how you arrived at your conclusions.

Your task in writing a critique is to turn your critical reading of a passage into a systematic evaluation in order to deepen your reader's (and your own) understanding of that passage. When you read a selection to critique, determine the following:

- What an author says
- How well the points are made
- What assumptions underlie the argument

- What issues are overlooked
- What implications can be drawn from such an assessment

When you write a critique, positive or negative, include the following:

- A fair and accurate summary of the passage
- Information and ideas from other sources (your reading or your personal experience and observations) if you think these are pertinent
- A statement of your agreement or disagreement with the author, backed by specific examples and clear logic
- A clear statement of your own assumptions

Remember that you bring to bear on any subject an entire set of assumptions about the world. Stated or not, these assumptions underlie every evaluative comment you make. You therefore have an obligation, both to the reader and to yourself, to clarify your standards by making your assumptions explicit. Not only do your readers stand to gain by your forthrightness, but you do as well. The process of writing a critical assessment forces you to examine your own knowledge, beliefs, and assumptions. Ultimately, the critique is a way of learning about yourself—yet another example of the ways in which writing is useful as a tool for critical thinking.

How to Write Critiques

You may find it useful to organize a critique into five sections: introduction, summary, assessment of the presentation (on its own terms), your response to the presentation, and conclusion.

The box that follows offers guidelines for writing critiques. These guidelines do not constitute a rigid formula. Most professional authors write critiques that do not follow the structure outlined here. Until you are more confident and practiced in writing critiques, however, we suggest you follow these guidelines. They are meant not to restrict you, but rather to provide a workable sequence for writing critiques until a more fully developed set of experiences and authorial instincts are available to guide you.

GUIDELINES FOR WRITING CRITIQUES

- *Introduce.* Introduce both the passage under analysis and the author. State the author's main argument and the point(s) you intend to make about it.

  Provide background material to help your readers understand the relevance or appeal of the passage. This background material might include one or more of the following: an explanation of why the subject is of current interest; a reference to a possible controversy surrounding the subject of the passage or the passage itself; biographical information about the author; an account of the circumstances under which the passage was written; a reference to the intended audience of the passage.

- *Summarize.* Summarize the author's main points, making sure to state the author's purpose for writing.

- *Assess the presentation.* Evaluate the validity of the author's presentation, distinct from your points of agreement or disagreement. Comment on the author's success in achieving his or her purpose by reviewing three or four specific points. You might base your review on one or more of the following criteria:

  Is the information accurate?

  Is the information significant?

  Has the author defined terms clearly?

  Has the author used and interpreted information fairly?

  Has the author argued logically?

- *Respond to the presentation.* Now it is your turn to respond to the author's views. With which views do you agree? With which do you disagree? Discuss your reasons for agreement and disagreement, when possible tying these reasons to assumptions—both the author's and your own. Where necessary, draw on outside sources to support your ideas.

- *Conclude.* State your conclusions about the overall validity of the piece—your assessment of the author's success at achieving his or her aims and your reactions to the author's views. Remind the reader of the weaknesses and strengths of the passage.

DEMONSTRATION: CRITIQUE

The critique that follows is based on Charles Krauthammer's op-ed piece "The Moon We Left Behind," which we have already begun to examine. In this formal critique, you will see that it is possible to agree with an author's main point, at least provisionally, yet disagree with other elements of the argument. Critiquing a different selection, you could just as easily accept the author's facts and figures but reject the conclusion he draws from them. As long as you carefully articulate the author's assumptions and your own, explaining in some detail your agreement and disagreement, the critique is yours to take in whatever direction you see fit.

Let's summarize the preceding sections by returning to the core questions that guide critical reading. You will see how, when applied to Charles Krauthammer's argument, they help to set up a critique.

To What Extent Does the Author Succeed in His or Her Purpose?

To answer this question, you will need to know the author's purpose. Krauthammer wrote "The Moon We Left Behind" to persuade his audience that manned space flight must be supported. He makes his case in three ways: (1) he attacks the Obama administration's decision to "retreat" from the moon—i.e., to end NASA's manned space program; (2) he argues for the continuation of this program; and (3) he rebuts criticisms of the program. He aims to achieve this purpose by unfavorably comparing President Obama to President Kennedy, who challenged the nation to put a man on the moon within a decade; by arguing that we should return to the moon for "the wonder and glory of it"; and by challenging the claims that (a) we need first to fix the problems on earth and that (b) we can't afford such a program. One of the main tasks of the writer of a critique of Krauthammer is to explain the extent to which Krauthammer has achieved his purpose.

To What Extent Do You Agree with the Author? Evaluate Assumptions

Krauthammer's argument rests upon two assumptions: (1) it is an essential characteristic of humankind to explore—and going to the moon was a great and worthwhile example of exploration; and (2) inspiring deeds are worth our expense and sacrifice—and thus continuing NASA's manned program and returning to the moon is worth our time, effort, and money. One who critiques Krauthammer must determine the extent to which she or he shares these assumptions. The writer of the model critique does, in fact, share Krauthammer's first assumption while expressing doubt about the second.

One must also determine the persuasiveness of Krauthammer's arguments for returning to the moon, as well as the persuasiveness of his counterarguments to those who claim this program is too impractical and too expensive. The writer of the model critique believes that Krauthammer's arguments are generally persuasive, even (in the conclusion) judging them "compelling." On the other hand, the critique ends on a neutral note—taking into account the problems with Krauthammer's arguments.

Remember that you don't need to agree with an author to believe that he or she has succeeded in his or her purpose. You may well admire how cogently and forcefully an author has argued without necessarily accepting her position. Conversely, you may agree with a particular author while acknowledging that he has not made a very strong case—and perhaps has even made a flawed one—for his point of view. For example, you may heartily approve of the point Krauthammer is making— that the United States should return to the moon. At the same time, you may find problematic the substance of his arguments and/or his strategy for arguing, particularly the dismissive manner in which he refers to the U.S. efforts in space over the last forty years:

> To be more precise: almost 40 years spent in low Earth orbit studying, well, zero-G nausea and sundry cosmic mysteries. We've done it with the most beautiful, intricate, complicated— and ultimately, hopelessly impractical—machine ever built by man: the space shuttle. We turned this magnificent bird into a truck for hauling goods and people to a tinkertoy we call the international space station.

Perhaps you support Krauthammer's position but find his sarcasm distasteful. That said, these two major questions for critical analysis (whether or not the author has been successful in his purpose and the extent to which you agree with the author's assumptions and arguments) are related. You will typically conclude that an author whose arguments have failed to persuade you has not succeeded in her purpose.

The selections you are likely to critique will be those, like Krauthammer's, that argue a specific position. Indeed, every argument you read is an invitation to agree or disagree. It remains only for you to speak up and justify your own position.

MODEL CRITIQUE

Harlan 1

Andrew Harlan

Professor Rose Humphreys

Writing 2

11 January 2011

A Critique of Charles Krauthammer's
"The Moon We Left Behind"

1   In his 1961 State of the Union address, President John F. Kennedy issued a stirring challenge: "that this nation

should commit itself to achieving the goal, before this decade is out, of landing a man on the Moon and returning him safely to the Earth." At the time, Kennedy's proposal seemed like science fiction. Even the scientists and engineers of the National Aeronautics and Space Administration (NASA) who were tasked with the job didn't know how to meet Kennedy's goal. Spurred, however, partly by a unified national purpose and partly by competition with the Soviet Union, which had beaten the United States into space with the first artificial satellite in 1957, the Apollo program to land men on the moon was launched. On July 20, 1969 Kennedy's challenge was met when Apollo 11 astronauts Neil Armstrong and Buzz Aldrin landed their lunar module on the Sea of Tranquility.

2   During the next few years, five more Apollo flights landed on the moon. In all, twelve Americans walked on the lunar surface; some even rode on a 4-wheeled "Rover," a kind of lunar dune buggy. But in December 1972 the Apollo program was cancelled. Since that time, some 40 years ago, humans have frequently returned to space, but none have returned to the moon. In February 2010 President Obama ended NASA's moon program, transferring responsibility for manned space exploration to private industry and re-focusing the government's resources on technological development and innovation. The administration had signaled its intentions earlier, in 2009. In July of that year, in an apparent attempt to rouse public opinion against the President's revised priorities for space exploration, Charles Krauthammer wrote "The Moon We Left Behind." It is these revised priorities that are the focus of his op-ed piece, a lament for the end of lunar exploration and a powerful, if flawed, critique of the administration's decision.

3   Trained as a doctor and a psychiatrist, Charles
Krauthammer is a prominent conservative columnist who
has won the Pulitzer Prize for his political commentary.
Krauthammer begins and ends his op-ed with expres-
sions of dismay and anger at "America's abandonment of
the moon." He unfavorably compares the current president, Barack Obama, with the "vigorous young" John F.
Kennedy, in terms of their support for manned space exploration. It is inconceivable to Krauthammer that a program
that achieved such technical glories and fired the imaginations of millions in so short a span of time has fallen into
such decline.

4   Krauthammer anticipates the objections to his plea
to keep America competitive in manned space exploration and to return to the moon. We have problems enough
on earth, critics will argue. His answer: If we waited to
solve these perennial problems before continuing human
progress, "we'd still be living in caves." Concerning the
expense of continuing the space program, Krauthammer
argues that a fraction of the funds being "showered" on the
government's stimulus programs (some $1 trillion) would
be sufficient to support a viable space program. And as for
practicality, he dismisses the idea that we need a practical
reason to return to the moon. "We go," he argues, "for the
wonder and glory of it. Or, to put it less grandly, for its
immense possibilities." Ultimately, Krauthammer urges us
to turn away from our mundane preoccupations and look
up at the moon where humans once walked. How could
Americans have gone so far, he asks, only to retreat?

5   In this opinion piece, Charles Krauthammer offers a
powerful, inspiring defense of the American manned space
program; and it's hard not to agree with him that our voy

Harlan 4

ages to the moon captured the imagination and admiration of the world and set a new standard for scientific and technical achievement. Ever since that historic day in July 1969, people have been asking, "If we can land a man on the moon, why can't we [fill in your favorite social or political challenge]?" In a way, the fact that going to the moon was not especially practical made the achievement even more admirable: we went not for gain but rather to explore the unknown, to show what human beings, working cooperatively and exercising their powers of reason and their genius in design and engineering, can accomplish when sufficiently challenged. "We go," Krauthammer reminds us, "for the wonder and glory of it . . . for its immense possibilities."

6   And what's wrong with that? For a relatively brief historical moment, Americans, and indeed the peoples of the world, came together in pride and anticipation as Apollo 11 sped toward the moon and, days later, as the lunar module descended to the surface. People collectively held their breaths after an oxygen tank explosion disabled Apollo 13 on the way to the moon and as the astronauts and Mission Control guided the spacecraft to a safe return. A renewed moon program might similarly help to reduce divisions among people—or at least among Americans—and highlight the reality that we are all residents of the same planet, with more common interests (such as protecting the environment) than is often apparent from our perennial conflicts. Krauthammer's praise of lunar exploration and its benefits is so stirring that many who do not accept his conclusions may share his disappointment and indignation at its demise.

7   "The Moon We Left Behind" may actually underestimate the practical aspects of moon travel. "Any

Harlan 5

technological return," Krauthammer writes, "is a bonus,
not a reason." But so many valuable bonuses have emerged
from space flight and space exploration that the practical
offshoots of lunar exploration may in fact be a valid reason
to return to the moon. For instance, the technology developed from the special requirements of space travel has found
application in health and medicine (breast cancer detection,
laser angioplasty), industrial productivity and manufacturing technology, public safety (radiation hazard detectors,
emergency rescue cutters), and transportation (studless
winter tires, advanced lubricants, aids to school bus design)
("NASA Spinoffs"). A renewed moon program would also
be practical in providing a huge employment stimulus to
the economy. According to the NASA Langley Research
Center, "At its peak, the Apollo program employed 400,000
people and required the support of over 20,000 industrial
firms and universities" ("Apollo Program"). Returning to
the moon would create comparable numbers of jobs in aero-
space engineering, computer engineering, biology, general
engineering, and meteorology, along with hosts of support
jobs, from accounting to food service to office automation
specialists ("NASA Occupations").

8

    Krauthammer's emotional call may be stirring, but he dis-
misses too quickly some of the practical arguments against
a renewed moon program. He appears to assume a degree of
political will and public support for further lunar exploration
that simply does not exist today. First, public support may be
lacking—for legitimate reasons. It is not as if with a renewed
lunar program we would be pushing boundaries and exploring the unknown: we would not be *going* to the moon; we
would be *returning* to the moon. A significant percentage

of the public, after considering the matter, may reasonably
conclude: "Been there, done that." They may think, correctly
or not, that we should set our sights elsewhere rather than
collecting more moon rocks or taking additional stunning
photographs from the lunar surface. Whatever practical benefits can be derived from going to the moon, many (if not all)
have already been achieved. It would not be at all unreasonable for the public, even a public that supports NASA funding, to say, "Let's move on to other goals."

9   Second, Krauthammer's argument that poverty and
disease and social ills will always be with us is politically
flawed. This country faces financial pressures more serious
than those at any other time since the Great Depression;
and real, painful choices are being made by federal, state,
and local officials about how to spend diminished tax
dollars. The "vigorous young" JFK, launching the moon
program during a time of expansion and prosperity, faced
no such restrictions. Krauthammer's dismissal of ongoing
poverty and other social ills is not likely to persuade elected
representatives who are shuttering libraries, closing fire sta-
tions, ending unemployment benefits, and curtailing medical services. Nor will a public that is enduring these cuts be
impressed by Krauthammer's call to "wonder and glory."
Accurately or not, the public is likely to see the matter in
terms of choices between a re-funded lunar program (nice,
but optional) and renewed jobless benefits (essential). Not
many politicians, in such distressed times, would be willing
to go on record by voting for "nice" over "essential"—not
if they wanted to keep their jobs.

10   Finally, it's surprising—and philosophically inconsistent—
for a conservative like Krauthammer, who believes in

Harlan 7

a smaller, less free-spending government, to be complaining about the withdrawal of massive government support
for a renewed moon program. After all, the government
hasn't banned moon travel; it has simply turned over such
projects to private industry. If lunar exploration and other
space flights appear commercially viable, there's nothing to
prevent private companies and corporations from pursuing
their own programs.

11   In "The Moon We Left Behind," Charles Krauthammer
stirs the emotions with his call for the United States to return
to the moon; and, in terms of practical spinoffs, such a return
could benefit this country in many ways. Krauthammer's
argument is compelling, even if he too easily discounts the
financial and political problems that will pose real obstacles
to a renewed lunar program. Ultimately, what one thinks
of Krauthammer's call to renew moon exploration depends
on how one defines the human enterprise and the purpose
of collective agreement and collective effort—what we call
"government." To what extent should this purpose be to
solve problems in the here and now? To what extent should
it be to inquire and to push against the boundaries for the
sake of discovery and exploration, to learn more about who
we are and about the nature of our universe? There have
always been competing demands on national budgets and
more than enough problems to justify spending every tax
dollar on problems of poverty, social justice, crime, education, national security, and the like. Krauthammer argues that
if we are to remain true to our spirit of inquiry, we cannot
ignore the investigation of space because scientific and technological progress is also a human responsibility. He argues
that we can—indeed, we must—do both: look to our needs

Harlan 8

here at home and also dream and explore. But the public may
not find his argument convincing.

Works Cited

"Apollo Program." *Apollo Program HSF*. National
    Aeronautics and Space Administration, 2 July 2009.
    Web. 16 Sept. 2010.

Harwood, William. "Obama Kills Moon Program, Endorses
    Commercial Space." *Spaceflight Now*. Spaceflight
    Now, 1 Feb. 2010. Web. 13 Sept. 2010.

Kennedy, John F. "Rice University Speech." 12 Sept. 1962.
    Public Papers of the Presidents of the United States.
    Vol. 1., 1962. 669–70. Print.

_____. "Special Message to the Congress on Urgent
    National Needs." *John F. Kennedy Presidential Library
    and Museum*. John F. Kennedy Presidential Library and
    Museum, 25 May 1961. Web. 14 Sept. 2010.

Krauthammer, Charles. "The Moon We Left Behind."
    Washington Post 17 July 2009: A17. Print.

"NASA Occupations." *Nasajobsoccupations*. National
    Aeronautics and Space Administration, 28 July 2009.
    Web. 12 Sept. 2010.

"NASA Spinoffs: Bringing Space Down to Earth." *The
    Ultimate Space Place*. National Aeronautics and Space
    Administration, 2 Feb. 2004. Web. 18 Sept. 2010.

CRITICAL READING FOR CRITIQUE

- *Use the tips from "Critical Reading for Summary" in
  Chapter 1.* Remember to examine the context; note the
  title and subtitle; identify the main point; identify the

subpoints; break the reading into sections; distinguish between points, examples, and counterarguments; watch for transitions within and between paragraphs; and read actively.

- *Establish the writer's primary purpose in writing.* Is the piece meant primarily to inform, persuade, or entertain?
- *Evaluate informative writing. Use these criteria (among others):*

  Accuracy of information

  Significance of information

  Fair interpretation of information

- *Evaluate persuasive writing. Use these criteria (among others):*

  Clear definition of terms

  Fair use and interpretation of information

  Logical reasoning

- *Evaluate writing that entertains. Use these criteria (among others):*

  Interesting characters

  Believable action, plot, and situations

  Communication of theme

  Use of language

- *Decide whether you agree or disagree with the writer's ideas, position, or message.* Once you have determined the extent to which an author has achieved his or her purpose, clarify your position in relation to the writer's.

The Strategy of the Critique

- Paragraphs 1 and 2 of the model critique introduce the topic. They provide a context by way of a historical review of America's lunar-exploration program from 1962 to 1972, leading up to the president's decision to scrub plans for a return to the moon. The two-paragraph introduction also provides a context for Krauthammer's—and the world's—admiration for the stunning achievement of the Apollo program. The second paragraph ends with the thesis of the critique, the writer's overall assessment of Krauthammer's essay.

- Paragraphs 3–4 introduce Krauthammer and summarize his arguments.
  - Paragraph 3 provides biographical information about Krauthammer and describes his disappointment and indignation at "America's abandonment of the moon."
  - Paragraph 4 treats Krauthammer's anticipated objections to the continuation of the manned space program and rebuttals to these objections.

- Paragraphs 5, 6, and 7 support Krauthammer's argument.
  - Paragraphs 5 and 6 begin the writer's evaluation, focusing on the reasons that Krauthammer finds so much to admire in the lunar-exploration program. Most notably: it was a stunning technological achievement that brought the people of the world together (if only briefly). The writer shares this admiration.
  - Paragraph 7 indirectly supports Krauthammer by pointing out that even though he downplays the practical benefits of lunar exploration, the space program has yielded numerous practical technological spinoffs.

- Paragraphs 8–10 focus on the problems with Krauthammer's argument.
  - In paragraph 8, the writer points out that there is little public support for returning to the moon, a goal that many people will see as already accomplished and impractical for the immediate future.
  - Paragraph 9 argues that Krauthammer underestimates the degree to which an electorate worried about skyrocketing deficits and high unemployment would object to taxpayer dollars being used to finance huge government spending on a renewed lunar program.

- Paragraph 10 points out how surprising it is that a conservative like Krauthammer would advocate a government-financed manned space program when the same goal could be accomplished by private enterprise.

- Paragraph 11 concludes the critique, summing up the chief strengths and weaknesses of Krauthammer's argument and pointing out that readers' positions will be determined by their views on the "human enterprise" and the purpose of government. How do we balance our "human responsibility" for the expansion of knowledge and technology with the competing claims of education, poverty, crime, and national security?

3
Synthesis

WHAT IS A SYNTHESIS?

A *synthesis* is a written discussion that draws on two or more sources. It follows that your ability to write syntheses depends on your ability to infer relationships among sources like these:

- Essays
- Fiction
- Interviews
- Articles
- Lectures
- Visual media

This process is nothing new for you because you infer relationships all the time—say, between something you've read in the newspaper and something you've seen for yourself, or between the teaching styles of your favorite and least favorite instructors. In fact, if you've written research papers, you've already written syntheses.

In a *synthesis*, you make explicit the relationships that you have inferred among separate sources.

Summary and Critique as a Basis for Synthesis

The skills you've already learned and practiced in the previous two chapters will be vital in writing syntheses. Before you're in a position to draw relationships between two or more sources, you must understand what those sources say; you must be able to *summarize* those sources. Readers will frequently benefit from at least partial summaries of sources in your synthesis essays. At the same time, you must go beyond summary to make judgments—judgments based on your *critical reading* of your sources: what conclusions you've drawn about the quality and validity of these sources, whether you agree or disagree with the points made in your sources, and why you agree or disagree.

Inference as a Basis for Synthesis: Moving Beyond Summary and Critique

In a synthesis, you go beyond the critique of individual sources to determine the relationships among them. Is the information in source B, for example, an extended illustration of the generalizations in source A? Would it be useful to compare and contrast source C with source B? Having read and considered sources A, B, and C, can you infer something else—in other words, D (not a source, but your own idea)?

Because a synthesis is based on two or more sources, you will need to be selective when choosing information from each. It would be neither possible nor desirable, for instance, to discuss in a ten-page paper on the American Civil War every point that the authors of two books make about their subject. What you as a writer must do is select from each source the ideas and information that best allow you to achieve your purpose.

PURPOSE

Your purpose in reading source materials and then drawing on them to write your own material is often reflected in the wording of an assignment. For instance, consider the following assignments on the Civil War:

American History: Evaluate the author's treatment of the origins of the Civil War.

Economics: Argue the following proposition, in light of your readings: "The Civil War was fought not for reasons of moral principle but for reasons of economic necessity."

Government: Prepare a report on the effects of the Civil War on Southern politics

Mass Communications: Discuss how the use of photography during the Civil War may have affected the perceptions of the war by Northerners living in industrial cities.

Literature: Select two Southern writers of the twentieth century whose work you believe was influenced by the divisive effects of the Civil War. Discuss the ways this influence is apparent in a novel or a group of short stories written by each author. The works should not be *about* the Civil War.

Applied Technology: Compare and contrast the technology of warfare available in the 1860s with the technology available a century earlier.

Each of these assignments creates a particular purpose for writing. Having located sources relevant to your topic, you would select for possible use in a paper only the parts of those sources that helped you in fulfilling this purpose. And how you used those parts—how you related them to other material from other sources—would also depend on your purpose.

Example: Same Sources, Different Uses

If you were working on the government assignment, you might draw on the same source as a student working on the literature assignment by referring to Robert Penn Warren's novel *All the King's Men,* about Louisiana politics in the early part of the twentieth century. But because the purposes of the two assignments are different, you and the other student would make different uses of this source. The parts or aspects of the novel that you find worthy of detailed analysis might be mentioned only in passing—or not at all—by the other student.

WHERE DO WE FIND WRITTEN SYNTHESES?

Here are just a few of the types of writing that involve synthesis:

Academic Writing

- **Analysis papers** synthesize and apply several related theoretical approaches.
- **Research papers** synthesize multiple sources.
- **Argument papers** synthesize different points into a coherent claim or position.
- **Essay exams** demonstrate understanding of course material through comparing and contrasting theories, viewpoints, or approaches in a particular field.

Workplace Writing

- **Newspaper and magazine articles** synthesize primary and secondary sources.
- **Position papers and policy briefs** compare and contrast solutions for solving problems.
- **Business plans** synthesize ideas and proposals into one coherent plan.
- **Memos and letters** synthesize multiple ideas, events, and proposals into concise form.
- **Web sites** synthesize information from various sources to present in Web pages and related links.

USING YOUR SOURCES

Your purpose determines not only what parts of your sources you will use but also how you will relate those parts to one another. Since the very essence of synthesis is the combining of information and ideas, you must have some basis on which to combine them. *Some relationships among the material in your sources must make them worth synthesizing.* It follows that the better able you are to discover such relationships, the better able you will be to use your sources in writing syntheses. Notice that the mass communications assignment requires you to draw a *cause-and-effect* relationship between photographs of the war and Northerners' perceptions of the war. The applied technology assignment requires you to *compare and contrast* state-of-the-art weapons technology in the eighteenth and nineteenth centuries. The economics assignment requires you to *argue* a proposition. In each case, *your purpose will determine how you relate your source materials to one another.*

Consider some other examples. You may be asked on an exam question or in the instructions for a paper to *describe* two or three approaches to prison reform during the past decade. You may be asked to *compare and contrast* one country's approach to imprisonment with another's. You may be asked to *develop an argument* of your own on this subject, based on your reading. Sometimes (when you are not given a specific assignment) you determine your own purpose: You are interested in exploring a particular subject; you are interested in making a case for one approach or another. In any event, your purpose shapes your essay. Your purpose determines which sources you research, which ones you use, which parts of them you use, at which points in your paper you use them, and in what manner you relate them to one another.

TYPES OF SYNTHESES: ARGUMENT AND EXPLANATORY

In this chapter we categorize syntheses into two main types: *argument and explanatory.* The easiest way to recognize the difference between the two types may be to consider the difference between a news article and an editorial on the same subject. For the most part, we'd say that the main purpose of the news article is to convey *information,* and that the main purpose of the editorial is to convey *opinion* or *interpretation.* Of course, this distinction is much too simplified: News articles often convey opinion or bias, sometimes subtly, sometimes openly; and editorials often convey unbiased information along with opinion. But as a practical matter we can generally agree on the distinction between a news article that primarily conveys information and an editorial that primarily conveys opinion. You should be able to observe this distinction in the selections shown here as Explanation and Argument.

Explanation: News Article from the New York Times

While Warning About Fat, U.S. Pushes Cheese Sales

By Michael Moss

November 6, 2010

1   Domino's Pizza was hurting early last year. Domestic sales had fallen, and a survey of big pizza chain customers left the company tied for the worst tasting pies.

2   Then help arrived from an organization called Dairy Management. It teamed up with Domino's to develop a new line of pizzas with 40 percent more cheese, and proceeded to devise and pay for a $12 million marketing campaign.

3   Consumers devoured the cheesier pizza, and sales soared by double digits. "This partnership is clearly working," Brandon Solano, the Domino's vice president for brand innovation, said in a statement to The New York Times.

4   But as healthy as this pizza has been for Domino's, one slice contains as much as two-thirds of a day's maximum recommended amount of saturated fat, which has been linked to heart disease and is high in calories.

5   And Dairy Management, which has made cheese its cause, is not a private business consultant. It is a marketing creation of the United States Department of Agriculture—the same agency at the center of a federal anti-obesity drive that discourages over-consumption of some of the very foods Dairy Management is vigorously promoting. ...

Argument: Editorial from the *Boston Globe*

Got Too Much Cheese?

By Derrick Z. Jackson

November 9, 2010

1   The chief executive of Dairy Management, Thomas Gallagher ... declined to be interviewed by the [New York] Times, but in a column last year in a trade publication, he wrote, "More cheese on pizza equals more cheese sales. In fact, if every pizza included one more ounce of cheese, we would see an additional 250 million pounds of cheese annually."

2   Emboldened by its success with cheese, Dairy Management is now reportedly working on bamboozling the public that chocolate milk is a sports recovery drink and persuading children to eat green beans by slathering them with cheese.

3   A year ago, at a joint press conference held by the USDA, the National Dairy Council and the National Football League to promote exercise, Gallagher said, "Child nutrition, particularly in schools, has been a cornerstone of the National Dairy Council for nearly a century. The program centers on youth taking the lead in changing the school environment."

4   The truth makes this a galling proclamation. Despite all the nutrition initiatives launched by the Obama administration, the cornerstone of federal policy continues to clog the nation's arteries, making a mockery of programs boasting how youth can take the lead. What is a cornerstone for the USDA is a gravestone for nutrition.

We'll say, for the sake of convenience, that the news article *explains* the contradictory messages on nutrition that the federal government is communicating and that the editorial *argues* that the contradiction is damaging. This important distinction between explanation and argument extends beyond the news to other materials you might consult while doing research. Consider a second set of passages:

What Are Genetically Modified (GM) Foods?

Genetically Modified Foods and Organisms

The United States Department of Energy

November 5, 2008

1   Combining genes from different organisms is known as recombinant DNA technology, and the resulting organism is said to be "genetically modified," "genetically engineered," or "transgenic." GM products (current or those in development) include medicines and vaccines, foods and food ingredients, feeds, and fibers.

2   Locating genes for important traits—such as those conferring insect resistance or desired nutrients—is one of the most limiting steps in the process. However, genome sequencing and discovery programs for hundreds of organisms are generating detailed maps along with data-analyzing technologies to understand and use them.

3   In 2006, 252 million acres of transgenic crops were planted in 22 countries by 10.3 million farmers. The majority of these crops were herbicide- and insect-resistant soybeans, corn, cotton, canola, and alfalfa. Other crops grown commercially or field-tested are a sweet potato resistant to a virus that could decimate most of the African harvest, rice with increased iron and vitamins that may alleviate chronic malnutrition in Asian countries, and a variety of plants able to survive weather extremes.

4   On the horizon are bananas that produce human vaccines against infectious diseases such as hepatitis B; fish that mature more quickly; cows that are resistant to bovine spongiform encephalopathy (mad cow disease); fruit and nut trees that yield years earlier, and plants that produce new plastics with unique properties.

Why a GM Freeze?

The GM Freeze Campaign

November 11, 2010

1   Genetic modification in food and farming raises many fundamental environmental, social, health and ethical concerns. There is increasing evidence of contamination of conventional crops and wild plants, and potential damage to wildlife. The effects on human health of eating these foods remain uncertain and some scientists are calling for much more rigorous safety testing. It is clear that further research into all these issues is vital. Furthermore the public has not been properly involved in decision making processes, despite strong public support for the precautionary approach to GM in the [United Kingdom] and the [European Union].

2   Much more time is needed to assess the need for and implications of using genetic modification in food and farming, in particular the increasing control of corporations who rely on patents to secure their future markets.

Both of these passages deal with the topic of genetically modified (GM) foods. The first is excerpted from a largely informational Web site published by the U.S. Department of Energy, which oversees the Human Genome Project, the government's ongoing effort to map gene sequences and apply that knowledge. We say the DOE account is "largely informational" because readers can find a great deal of information here about genetically modified foods. At the same time, however, the DOE explanation is subtly biased in favor of genetic modification: note the absence of any language raising questions about the ethics or safety of GM foods; note also the use of terms like "desired nutrients" and "insect resistance"—with their positive connotations. The DOE examples show GM foods in a favorable light, and the passage as a whole assumes the value and importance of genetic manipulation.

As we see in the second passage, however, that assumption is not shared by all. Excerpted from a Web site advocating a freeze on genetically modified crops, the second passage primarily argues against the ethics and safety of such manipulation, calling for more study before modified crops are released widely into the environment. At the same time, the selection provides potentially important explanatory materials: (1) the claim that there is "increasing evidence of contamination of conventional crops and wild plants, and potential damage to wildlife"; (2) the claim that corporations control GM crops, and potentially the food supply, through patents. We can easily and quickly confirm these claims through research; if confirmed, the information—which is nested in a primarily argumentative piece—could prove useful in a paper on GM foods.

So while it is fair to say that most writing can be broadly categorized as explanatory or argumentative, understand that in practice, many of the materials you read will be a mix: *primarily* one or the other but not altogether one or the other. It will be your job as an alert, critical reader to determine when authors are explaining or arguing—sometimes in the same sentence.

For instance, you might read the following in a magazine article: "The use of goats to manufacture anti-clotting proteins for humans in their milk sets a dangerous precedent." Perhaps you did not know that scientists have genetically manipulated goats (by inserting human genes) to create medicines. That much of the statement is factual. It is explanatory. Whether or not this fact "sets a dangerous precedent" is an argument. You could agree or not with the argument; but your views would not change the fact about the genetic manipulation of farm animals. Even within a single sentence, then, you must be alert to distinguishing between explanation and argument.

HOW TO WRITE SYNTHESES

Although writing syntheses can't be reduced to a lockstep method, it should help you to follow the guidelines listed in the box that follows.

GUIDELINES FOR WRITING SYNTHESES

- *Consider your purpose in writing.* What are you trying to accomplish in your paper? How will this purpose shape the way you approach your sources?
- *Select and carefully read your sources* according to your purpose. Then reread the passages, mentally summarizing each. Identify those aspects or parts of your sources that will help you fulfill your purpose. When rereading, *label* or *underline* the sources' main ideas, key terms, and any details you want to use in the synthesis.
- *Take notes on your reading.* In addition to labeling or underlining key points in the readings, you might write brief one- or two-sentence summaries of each source. This will help you in formulating your thesis statement and in choosing and organizing your sources later.
- *Formulate a thesis.* Your thesis is the main idea that you want to present in your synthesis. It should be expressed as a complete sentence. You might do some predrafting about the ideas discussed in the readings in order to help you work out a thesis. If you've written one-sentence summaries of the readings, looking over the summaries will help you to brainstorm connections between readings and to devise a thesis.

    When you write your synthesis drafts, you will need to consider where your thesis fits in your paper. Sometimes the thesis is the first sentence, but more often it is *the final sentence of the first paragraph.* If you are writing an *inductively arranged* synthesis (see the section on "Making a Claim: Formulate a Thesis" earlier in this chapter), the thesis sentence may not appear until the final paragraphs.
- *Decide how you will use your source material.* How will the information and the ideas in the passages help you fulfill your purpose?
- *Develop an organizational plan,* according to your thesis. How will you arrange your material? It is not necessary to prepare a formal outline. But you should have some plan

that will indicate the order in which you will present your material and the relationships among your sources.

- *Draft the topic sentences for the main sections.* This is an optional step, but you may find it a helpful transition from organizational plan to first draft.

- *Write the first draft* of your synthesis, following your organizational plan. Be flexible with your plan, however. Frequently, you will use an outline to get started. As you write, you may discover new ideas and make room for them by adjusting the outline. When this happens, reread your work frequently, making sure that your thesis still accounts for what follows and that what follows still logically supports your thesis.

- *Document your sources.* You must do this by crediting sources within the body of the synthesis—citing the author's last name and the page number from which the point was taken—and then providing full citation information in a list of "Works Cited" at the end. Don't open yourself to charges of plagiarism! (See the section on "Avoiding Plagiarism" in chapter 1.)

- *Revise your synthesis,* inserting transitional words and phrases where necessary. Make sure that the synthesis reads smoothly, logically, and clearly from beginning to end. Check for grammatical correctness, punctuation, and spelling.

Note: The writing of syntheses is a recursive process, and you should accept a certain amount of backtracking and reformulating as inevitable. For instance, in developing an organizational plan (Step 6 of the procedure), you may discover a gap in your presentation that will send you scrambling for another source—back to Step 2. You may find that formulating a thesis and making inferences among sources occur simultaneously; indeed, inferences are often made before a thesis is formulated. Our recommendations for writing syntheses will give you a structure that will get you started. But be flexible in your

(Continued on next page)

> *approach; expect discontinuity and, if possible, be assured that*
> *through backtracking and reformulating, you will produce a*
> *coherent, well-crafted paper.*

THE ARGUMENT SYNTHESIS

An argument is an attempt to persuade a reader or listener that a particular and debatable claim is true. Writers argue in order to establish facts, to make statements of value, and to recommend policies. For instance, answering the question *Why do soldiers sometimes commit atrocities in wartime?* would involve making an argument. To develop this argument, researchers might conduct experiments, interview experts, collect historical evidence, and examine and interpret data. The researchers might then present their findings at professional conferences and in journals and books. The extent to which readers (or listeners) accept these findings will depend on the quality of the supporting evidence and the care with which the researchers have argued their case. What we are calling an argument *synthesis* draws upon evidence from a variety of sources in an attempt to persuade others of the truth or validity of a debatable claim.

By contrast, the explanatory synthesis is fairly modest in purpose. It emphasizes the sources themselves, not the writer's use of sources to persuade others. The writer of an explanatory synthesis aims to inform, not persuade. Here, for example, is a thesis devised for an explanatory synthesis on the ubiquity of cell phones in contemporary life:

> Cell phones make it possible for us to be always within reach, though many people would prefer *not* to be always within reach.

This thesis summarizes two viewpoints about the impact of cell phones on contemporary life, arguing neither for nor against either viewpoint.

An argument thesis, however, is *persuasive* in purpose. A writer working with the same source material might conceive and support an opposing thesis:

Cell phones have ruined our ability to be isolated, to be willfully *out of touch* with the rest of the world.

So the thesis for an argument synthesis is a claim about which reasonable people could disagree. It is a claim with which—given the right arguments—your audience might be persuaded to agree. The strategy of your argument synthesis is therefore to find and use convincing *support* for your *claim*.

The Elements of Argument: Claim, Support, and Assumption

One way of looking at an argument is to see it as an interplay of three essential elements: claim, support, and assumption. A *claim* is a proposition or conclusion that you are trying to prove. You prove this claim by using *support* in the form of fact, statistics, or expert opinion. Linking your supporting evidence to your claim is your *assumption* about the subject. This assumption, also called a *warrant* (as we've discussed in Chapter 2), is an underlying belief or principle about some aspect of the world and how it operates. By their nature, assumptions (which are often unstated) tend to be more general than either claims or supporting evidence.

Here are the essential elements of an argument advocating parental restriction of television viewing for high school students:

Claim
High school students should be restricted to no more than two hours of TV viewing per day.

Support
An important new study and the testimony of educational specialists reveal that students who watch more than two hours of TV a night have, on average, lower grades than those who watch less TV.

Assumption
Excessive TV viewing adversely affects academic performance.

As another example, here's an argumentative claim on the topic of computer-mediated communication (CMC)—a term sociologists use to describe online contacts among friends and family:

> CMC threatens to undermine human intimacy, connection, and ultimately community.

Here are the other elements of this argument:

Support

- People are spending increasing amounts of time in cyberspace: In 1998, the average Internet user spent over four hours per week online, a figure that more than tripled in the last decade.

- College health officials report that excessive Internet use threatens many college students' academic and psychological well-being.

- New kinds of relationships fostered on the Internet often pose challenges to pre-existing relationships.

Assumptions

- The communication skills used and the connections formed during Internet contact fundamentally differ from those used and formed during face-to-face contact.

- "Real" connection and a sense of community are sustained by face-to-face contact, not by Internet interactions.

For the most part, arguments should be constructed logically so that assumptions link evidence (supporting facts, statistics, and expert opinions) to claims. As we'll see, however, logic is only one component of effective arguments.

DEMONSTRATION: DEVELOPING AN ARGUMENT SYNTHESIS—BALANCING PRIVACY AND SAFETY IN THE WAKE OF VIRGINIA TECH

To demonstrate how to plan and draft an argument synthesis, let's suppose you are taking a course on Law and Society or Political Science or (from the Philosophy Department) Theories of Justice, and you find yourself considering the competing claims of privacy and public safety. The tension between these two highly prized values burst anew into public consciousness in 2007 after a mentally disturbed student at the Virginia Polytechnic Institute shot to death thirty-two fellow students and faculty members and injured seventeen more. Unfortunately, this incident was only the latest in a long history of mass killings at American schools.* It was later revealed that the shooter had a documented history of mental instability, but because of privacy rules, this information was not made available to university officials. Many people demanded to know why this information had not been shared with campus police or other officials so that Virginia Tech could have taken measures to protect members of the university community. Didn't the safety of those who were injured or killed outweigh the privacy of the shooter? At what point, if any, *does* the right to privacy outweigh the right to safety? What *should* the university have done before the killing started? Should federal and state laws on privacy be changed or even abandoned in the wake of this and other similar incidents?

Suppose, in preparing to write a paper on balancing privacy and safety, you located (among others) the following sources:

- *Mass Shootings at Virginia Tech, April 16, 2007: Report of the Review Panel Presented to Governor Kaine, Commonwealth of Virginia,* August 2007 (a report)

- "Virginia Tech Massacre Has Altered Campus Mental Health Systems" (a newspaper article)

- *The Family Educational Rights and Privacy Act (FERPA),* sec. 1232g (a federal statute)

Carefully read these sources (which follow), noting the kinds of evidence—facts, expert opinions, and statistics—you

---

*In 1966 a student at the University of Texas at Austin, shooting from the campus clock tower, killed 14 people and wounded 31. In 2006 a man shot and killed five girls at an Amish school in Lancaster, Pennsylvania.

could draw on to develop an *argument synthesis*. Some of these passages are excerpts only; in preparing your paper, you would draw on the entire articles, reports, and book chapters from which these passages were taken. And you would draw on more sources than these in your search for supporting materials (as the writer of the model synthesis has done). But these three sources provide a good introduction to the subject. Our discussion of how these passages can form the basis of an argument synthesis resumes immediately following the source readings.

Mass Shootings at Virginia Tech, April 16, 2007

Report of the Review Panel
Presented to Governor Kaine, Commonwealth
of Virginia, August 2007

The following passage leads off the official report of the Virginia Tech shootings by the panel appointed by Virginia Governor Tim Kaine to investigate the incident. The mission of the panel was "to provide an independent, thorough, and objective incident review of this tragic event, including a review of educational laws, policies and institutions, the public safety and health care procedures and responses, and the mental health delivery system." Panel members included the chair, Colonel Gerald Massenghill, former Virginia State Police Superintendent; Tom Ridge, former Director of Homeland Security and former governor of Pennsylvania; Gordon Davies; Dr. Roger L. Depue; Dr. Aradhana A. "Bela" Sood; Judge Diane Strickland; and Carol L. Ellis. The panel's Web site may be found at <http://www.vtreviewpanel.org/panel_info/>.

Summary of Key Findings

1 On April 16, 2007, Seung Hui Cho, an angry and disturbed student, shot to death 32 students and faculty of Virginia Tech, wounded 17 more, and then killed himself.

2   The incident horrified not only Virginians, but people across the United States and throughout the world.

3   Tim Kaine, Governor of the Commonwealth of Virginia, immediately appointed a panel to review the events leading up to this tragedy; the handling of the incidents by public safety officials,

emergency services providers, and the university; and the services subsequently provided to families, survivors, caregivers, and the community.

4   The Virginia Tech Review Panel reviewed several separate but related issues in assessing events leading to the mass shootings and their aftermath:

- The life and mental health history of Seung Hui Cho, from early childhood until the weeks before April 16.
- Federal and state laws concerning the privacy of health and education records.
- Cho's purchase of guns and related gun control issues.
- The double homicide at West Ambler Johnston (WAJ) residence hall and the mass shootings at Norris Hall, including the responses of Virginia Tech leadership and the actions of law enforcement officers and emergency responders.
- Emergency medical care immediately following the shootings, both onsite at Virginia Tech and in cooperating hospitals.
- The work of the Office of the Chief Medical Examiner of Virginia.
- The services provided for surviving victims of the shootings and others injured, the families and loved ones of those killed and injured, members of the university community, and caregivers.

5   The panel conducted over 200 interviews and reviewed thousands of pages of records, and reports the following major findings:

1. Cho exhibited signs of mental health problems during his childhood. His middle and high schools responded well to these signs and, with his parents' involvement, provided services to address his issues. He also received private psychiatric treatment and counseling for selective mutism and depression.

   In 1999, after the Columbine shootings, Cho's middle school teachers observed suicidal and homicidal ideations in his writings and recommended psychiatric counseling, which he received. It was at this point that he received medication for a short time. Although Cho's parents were aware that he was troubled at this time, they state they did not specifically know that he thought about homicide shortly after the 1999 Columbine school shootings.

2. During Cho's junior year at Virginia Tech, numerous incidents occurred that were clear warnings of mental instability. Although various individuals and departments within the university knew about each of these incidents, the university did not intervene effectively. No one knew all the information and no one connected all the dots.

3. University officials in the office of Judicial Affairs, Cook Counseling Center, campus police, the Dean of Students, and others explained their failures to communicate with one another or with Cho's parents by noting their belief that such communications are prohibited by the federal laws governing the privacy of health and education records. In reality, federal laws and their state counterparts afford ample leeway to share information in potentially dangerous situations.

4. The Cook Counseling Center and the university's Care Team failed to provide needed support and services to Cho during a period in late 2005 and early 2006. The system failed for lack of resources, incorrect interpretation of privacy laws, and passivity. Records of Cho's minimal treatment at Virginia Tech's Cook Counseling Center are missing.

5. Virginia's mental health laws are flawed and services for mental health users are inadequate. Lack of sufficient resources results in gaps in the mental health system including short term crisis stabilization and comprehensive outpatient services. The involuntary commitment process is challenged by unrealistic time constraints, lack of critical psychiatric data and collateral information, and barriers (perceived or real) to open communications among key professionals.

6. There is widespread confusion about what federal and state privacy laws allow. Also, the federal laws governing records of health care provided in educational settings are not entirely compatible with those governing other health records.

7. Cho purchased two guns in violation of federal law. The fact that in 2005 Cho had been judged to be a danger to himself and ordered to outpatient treatment made him ineligible to purchase a gun under federal law.

8. Virginia is one of only 22 states that report any information about mental health to a federal database used to conduct background checks on would-be gun purchasers. But Virginia law did not clearly require that persons such as Cho—who had been ordered into out-patient treatment but not committed to an institution—be reported to the database. Governor Kaine's executive order to report all persons involuntarily committed for outpatient treatment has temporarily addressed this ambiguity in state law. But a change is needed in the Code of Virginia as well.

9. Some Virginia colleges and universities are uncertain about what they are permitted to do regarding the possession of firearms on campus.

10. On April 16, 2007, the Virginia Tech and Blacksburg police departments responded quickly to the report of shootings at West Ambler Johnston residence hall, as did the Virginia Tech and Blacksburg rescue squads. Their responses were well coordinated.

11. The Virginia Tech police may have erred in prematurely concluding that their initial lead in the double homicide was a good one, or at least in conveying that impression to university officials while continuing their investigation. They did not take sufficient action to deal with what might happen if the initial lead proved erroneous. The police reported to the university emergency Policy Group that the "person of interest" probably was no longer on campus.

12. The VTPD erred in not requesting that the Policy Group issue a campus-wide notification that two persons had been killed and that all students and staff should be cautious and alert.

13. Senior university administrators, acting as the emergency Policy Group, failed to issue an all-campus notification about the WAJ killings until almost 2 hours had elapsed. University practice may have conflicted with written policies.

14. The presence of large numbers of police at WAJ led to a rapid response to the first 9-1-1 call that shooting had begun at Norris Hall.

15. Cho's motives for the WAJ or Norris Hall shootings are unknown to the police or the panel. Cho's writings and videotaped pronouncements do not explain why he struck when and where he did.

16. The police response at Norris Hall was prompt and effective, as was triage and evacuation of the wounded. Evacuation of others in the building could have been implemented with more care.

17. Emergency medical care immediately following the shootings was provided very effectively and timely both onsite and at the hospitals, although providers from different agencies had some difficulty communicating with one another. Communication of accurate information to hospitals standing by to receive the wounded and injured was somewhat deficient early on. An emergency operations center at Virginia Tech could have improved communications.

18. The Office of the Chief Medical Examiner properly discharged the technical aspects of its responsibility (primarily autopsies and identification of the deceased). Communication with families was poorly handled.

19. State systems for rapidly deploying trained professional staff to help families get information, crisis intervention, and referrals to a wide range of resources did not work.

20. The university established a family assistance center at The Inn at Virginia Tech, but it fell short in helping families and others for two reasons: lack of leadership and lack of coordination among service providers. University volunteers stepped in but were not trained or able to answer many questions and guide families to the resources they needed.

21. In order to advance public safety and meet public needs, Virginia's colleges and universities need to work together as a coordinated system of state-supported institutions.

6   As reflected in the body of the report, the panel has made more than 70 recommendations directed to colleges, universities, mental health providers, law enforcement officials, emergency service providers, lawmakers, and other public officials in Virginia and elsewhere.

Virginia Tech Massacre Has Altered Campus Mental Health Systems

This article, prepared by the Associated Press, is representative of numerous reports of how college administrators across the nation responded to the Virginia Tech killings. Many schools reviewed their existing policies on student privacy and communication and instituted new procedures. The article appeared in the Los Angeles Times on April 14, 2008.

1   The rampage carried out nearly a year ago by a Virginia Tech student who slipped through the mental health system has changed how American colleges reach out to troubled students.

2   Administrators are pushing students harder to get help, looking more aggressively for signs of trouble and urging faculty to speak up when they have concerns. Counselors say the changes are sending even more students their way, which is both welcome and a challenge, given that many still lack the resources to handle their growing workloads.

3   Behind those changes, colleges have edged away in the last year from decades-old practices that made student privacy paramount. Now, they are more likely to err on the side of sharing information—with the police, for instance, and parents—if there is any possible threat to community safety. But even some who say the changes are appropriate worry it could discourage students from seeking treatment.

4   Concerns also linger that the response to shooters like Seung-hui Cho at Virginia Tech and Steven Kazmierczak, who killed five others at Northern Illinois University, has focused excessively on boosting the capacity of campus police to respond to rare events. Such reforms may be worthwhile, but they don't address how to prevent such a tragedy in the first place.

5   It was last April 16, just after 7 a.m., that Cho killed two students in a Virginia Tech dormitory, the start of a shooting spree that continued in a classroom building and eventually claimed 33 lives, including his own.

6   Cho's behavior and writing had alarmed professors and administrators, as well as the campus police, and he had been

put through a commitment hearing where he was found to be potentially dangerous. But when an off-campus psychiatrist sent him back to the school for outpatient treatment, there was no follow-up to ensure that he got it.

7   People who work every day in the campus mental health field—counselors, lawyers, advocates and students at colleges around the country—say they have seen three major types of change since the Cho shootings:

8   Faculty are speaking up more about students who worry them. That's accelerating a trend of more demand for mental health services that was already under way before the Virginia Tech shootings.

9   Professors "have a really heightened level of fear and concern from the behavior that goes on around them," said Ben Locke, assistant director of the counseling center at Penn State University.

10   David Wallace, director of counseling at the University of Central Florida, said teachers are paying closer attention to violent material in writing assignments—warning bells that had worried Cho's professors.

11   "Now people are wondering, 'Is this something that could be more ominous?'" he said. "Are we talking about the Stephen Kings of the future or about somebody who's seriously thinking about doing something harmful?"

12   The downside is officials may be hypersensitive to any eccentricity. Says Susan Davis, an attorney who works in student affairs at the University of Virginia: "There's no question there's some hysteria and there's some things we don't need to see."

13   Changes are being made to privacy policies. In Virginia, a measure signed into law Wednesday by Gov. Tim Kaine requires colleges to bring parents into the loop when dependent students may be a danger to themselves or others.

14   Even before Virginia Tech, Cornell University had begun treating students as dependents of their parents unless told otherwise—an aggressive legal strategy that gives the school more leeway to contact parents with concerns without students' permission.

15   In Washington, meanwhile, federal officials are trying to clarify privacy guidelines so faculty won't hesitate to report potential threats.

16   "Nobody's throwing privacy out the window, but we are coming out of an era when individual rights were paramount on college campuses," said Brett Sokolow, who advises colleges on risk management. "What colleges are struggling with now is a better balance of those individual rights and community protections."

17   The big change since the Virginia Tech shootings, legal experts say, is colleges have shed some of their fear of violating the federal Family Educational Rights and Privacy Act.

18   Many faculty hadn't realized that the law applies only to educational records, not observations of classroom behavior, or that it contains numerous exceptions.

19   The stigma of mental illness, in some cases, has grown. "In general, the attention to campus mental health was desperately needed," said Alison Malmon, founder of the national Active Minds group. But some of the debate, she added, "has turned in a direction that does not necessarily support students."

20   All the talk of "threat assessments" and better-trained campus SWAT teams, she said, has distracted the public from the fact that the mentally ill rarely commit violence—especially against others.

21   "I know that, for many students, it made them feel more stigmatized," Malmon said. "It made them more likely to keep their mental health history silent."

22   Sokolow, the risk consultant for colleges, estimated in the aftermath of the Virginia Tech and NIU shootings, the schools he works with spent $25 on police and communications for every $1 on mental health. Only recently has he seen a shift.

23   "Campuses come to me, they want me to help them start behavioral intervention systems," Sokolow said. "Then they go to the president to get the money and, oh, well, the money went into the door locks."

24   Phone messaging systems and security are nice, he said, but "there is nothing about text-messaging that is going to prevent violence."

The Family Educational Rights and Privacy Act (FERPA)

United States Code
Title 20. Education
CHAPTER 31. General Provisions
Concerning Education
§ 1232g. Family Educational
and Privacy Rights

*Following are excerpts from the Family Educational Rights and Privacy Act
(FERPA), the federal law enacted in 1974 that governs restrictions on the
release of student educational records. FERPA provides for the withholding
of federal funds to educational institutions that violate its provisions, and it
is the federal guarantor of the privacy rights of post-secondary students.*

(1) (A) No funds shall be made available under any applicable program to any educational agency or institution which has a
policy of denying, or which effectively prevents, the parents of
students who are or have been in attendance at a school of such
agency or at such institution, as the case may be, the right to
inspect and review the education records of their children. If any
material or document in the education record of a student
includes information on more than one student, the parents of
one of such students shall have the right to inspect and review
only such part of such material or document as relates to such
student or to be informed of the specific information contained
in such part of such material. Each educational agency or institution shall establish appropriate procedures for the granting of a
request by parents for access to the education records of their
children within a reasonable period of time, but in no case more
than forty-five days after the request has been made....

(C) The first sentence of subparagraph (A) shall not operate
to make available to students in institutions of postsecondary
education the following materials:

      (i) financial records of the parents of the student or any
          information contained therein;

    (ii) confidential letters and statements of recommenda-
tion, which were placed in the education records prior
to January 1, 1975, if such letters or statements are
not used for purposes other than those for which
they were specifically intended;

   (iii) if the student has signed a waiver of the student's right
of access under this subsection in accordance with
subparagraph (D), confidential recommendations—

       (I) respecting admission to any educational agency or
institution,

     (II) respecting an application for employment, and

    (III) respecting the receipt of an honor or honorary
recognition.

(B) The term "education records" does not include—

    (i) records of instructional, supervisory, and administrative
personnel and educational personnel ancillary thereto
which are in the sole possession of the maker thereof
and which are not accessible or revealed to any other
person except a substitute;

   (ii) records maintained by a law enforcement unit of the
educational agency or institution that were created
by that law enforcement unit for the purpose of law
enforcement;

  (iii) in the case of persons who are employed by an educational agency or institution but who are not in
attendance at such agency or institution, records
made and maintained in the normal course of business which relate exclusively to such person in that
person's capacity as an employee and are not available for use for any other purpose; or

  (iv) records on a student who is eighteen years of age or
older, or is attending an institution of postsecondary
education, which are made or maintained by a physician, psychiatrist, psychologist, or other recognized
professional or paraprofessional acting in his professional or paraprofessional capacity, or assisting in that

capacity, and which are made, maintained, or used only in connection with the provision of treatment to the student, and are not available to anyone other than persons providing such treatment, except that such records can be personally reviewed by a physician or other appropriate professional of the student's choice....

(h) Certain disciplinary action information allowable. Nothing in this section shall prohibit an educational agency or institution from—

   (1) including appropriate information in the education record of any student concerning disciplinary action taken against such student for conduct that posed a significant risk to the safety or well-being of that student, other students, or other members of the school community; or

(2) disclosing such information to teachers and school officials, including teachers and school officials in other schools, who have legitimate educational interests in the behavior of the student.

Consider Your Purpose

Your specific purpose in writing an argument synthesis is crucial. What exactly you want to do will affect your claim and how you organize the evidence. Your purpose may be clear to you before you begin research, or it may not emerge until after you have completed your research. Of course, the sooner your purpose is clear to you, the fewer wasted motions you will make. On the other hand, the more you approach research as an exploratory process, the likelier that your conclusions will emerge from the sources themselves rather than from preconceived ideas. Each new writing project will have its own rhythm in this regard. Be flexible in your approach: through some combination of preconceived structures and invigorating discoveries, you will find your way to the source materials that will yield a promising paper.

Let's say that while reading these seven (and additional) sources on the debate about campus safety and student privacy, you share the outrage of many who blamed the university (and the federal privacy laws on which it relied) for not using the available information in a way that might have spared the lives of those who died. Perhaps you also blame the legislators who wrote the privacy laws for being more concerned about the confidentiality of the mental health records of the individual person than with the safety of the larger college population. Perhaps, you conclude, society has gone too far in valuing privacy more than it appears to value safety.

On the other hand, in your own role as a student, perhaps you share the high value placed on the privacy of sensitive information about yourself. After all, one of the functions of higher education is to foster students' independence as they make the transition from adolescence to adulthood. You can understand that many students like yourself might not want their parents or others to know details about academic records or disciplinary measures, much less information about therapy sought and undertaken at school. Historically, in the decades since the university officially stood *in loco parentis*—in place of parents—students have struggled hard to win the same civil liberties and rights (including the right to privacy) of their elders.

Further, you may wonder whether federal privacy laws do in fact forbid the sharing of information about potentially dangerous students when the health and safety of others are at stake. A little research may begin to confirm your doubts whether Virginia Tech officials were really as helpless as they claimed they were.

Your purpose in writing, then, emerges from these kinds of responses to the source materials you find.

Making a Claim: Formulate a Thesis

As we indicated in the introduction to this chapter, one useful way of approaching an argument is to see it as making a *claim*. A claim is a proposition, a conclusion you have made, that you are trying to prove or demonstrate. If your purpose is to argue that we should work to ensure campus safety without enacting restrictive laws that overturn the hard-won privacy rights of students, then that claim (generally expressed in one-sentence form as a *thesis*) is at the heart of your argument. You will draw support from your sources as you argue logically for your claim.

Not every piece of information in a source is useful for supporting a claim. You must read with care and select the opinions, facts, and statistics that best advance your position. You may even find yourself drawing support from sources that make claims entirely different from your own. For example, in researching the subject of student privacy and campus safety, you may come across editorials arguing that in the wake of the Virginia Tech shootings, student privacy rights should be greatly restricted. Perhaps you will find information in these sources to help support your own contrary arguments.

You might use one source as part of a *counterargument*—an argument opposing your own—so that you can demonstrate its weaknesses and, in the process, strengthen your own claim. On the other hand, the author of one of your sources may be so convincing in supporting a claim that you adopt it yourself, either partially or entirely. The point is that *the argument is in your hands.* You must devise it yourself and use your sources in ways that will support the claim you present in your thesis.

You may not want to divulge your thesis until the end of the paper, thereby drawing the reader along toward your conclusion, allowing the thesis to flow naturally out of the argument and the evidence on which it is based. If you do this, you are working *inductively.* Or you may wish to be more direct and (after an introduction) *begin* with your thesis, following the thesis statement with evidence and reasoning to support it. If you do this, you are working *deductively.* In academic papers, deductive arguments are far more common than inductive ones.

Based on your reactions to reading sources—and perhaps also on your own inclinations as a student—you may find yourself essentially in sympathy with the approach to privacy taken by one of the schools covered in your sources, M.I.T. At the same time, you may feel that M.I.T.'s position does not demonstrate sufficient concern for campus safety and that

Cornell's position, on the other hand, restricts student privacy too much. Perhaps most important, you conclude that we don't need to change the law because, if correctly interpreted, the law already incorporates a good balance between privacy and safety. After a few tries, you develop this thesis:

> In responding to the Virginia Tech killings, we should resist rolling back federal rules protecting student privacy; for as long as college officials effectively respond to signs of trouble, these rules already provide a workable balance between privacy and public safety.

Decide How You Will Use Your Source Material

Your claim commits you to (1) arguing that student privacy should remain protected, and (2) demonstrating that federal law already strikes a balance between privacy and public safety. The sources (some provided here, some located elsewhere) offer information and ideas—evidence—that will allow you to support your claim. The excerpt from the official report on the Virginia Tech shootings reveals a finding that school officials failed to correctly interpret federal privacy rules and failed to "intervene effectively." The article "Virginia Tech Massacre Has Altered Campus Mental Health Systems" outlines some of the ways that campuses around the country have instituted policy changes regarding troubled students and privacy in the wake of Virginia Tech. And the excerpt from the *Family Educational Rights and Privacy Act (FERPA)*, the federal law, reveals that restrictions on revealing students' confidential information have a crucial exception for "the safety or well-being of . . . students, or other members of the school community." (These and several other sources not included in this chapter will be cited in the model argument paper.)

Develop an Organizational Plan

Having established your overall purpose and your claim, having developed a thesis (which may change as you write and revise the paper), and having decided how to draw upon your source materials, how do you logically organize your paper? In many cases, a well-written thesis will suggest an organization. Thus, the first part of your paper will deal with the debate over rolling back student privacy. The second part will argue that as long as educational institutions behave proactively—that is, as long as they actively seek to help troubled students and foster campus safety—existing federal rules already preserve a balance between privacy and safety. Sorting through your material and categorizing it by topic and subtopic, you might compose the following outline:

I. Introduction. Recap Virginia Tech shooting. College officials, citing privacy rules, did not act on available info about shooter with history of mental problems.

II. Federal rules on privacy. Subsequent debate over balance between privacy and campus safety. Pendulum now moving back toward safety. *Thesis.*

III. Developments in student privacy in recent decades.
   A. Doctrine of *in loco parentis* defines college-student relationship.
   B. Movement away from *in loco parentis* begins in 1960s, in context not only of student rights but also broader civil rights struggles of the period.
   C. FERPA, enacted 1974, establishes new federal rules protecting student privacy.

IV. Arguments *against* student privacy.
   A. In wake of Virginia Tech, many blame FERPA protections and college officials, believing privacy rights have been taken too far, putting campus community at risk.
   B. Cornell rolls back some FERPA privacy rights.

V. Arguments *for* student privacy.
   A. M.I.T. strongly defends right to privacy.
   B. Problem is not federal law but incorrect interpretation of federal law. FERPA provides health and safety exceptions. Virginia Tech officials erred in citing FERPA for not sharing info about shooter earlier.

   C. University of Kentucky offers good balance between
      competing claims of privacy and safety.
      1. watch lists of troubled students
      2. threat assessment groups
      3. open communication among university officials
VI. Conclusion.
   A. Virginia Tech incident was an instance of a legal issue
      students will encounter in the broader world: rights of
      the individual vs. rights of the larger group.
   B. Virginia Tech incident was tragic but should not cause
      us to overturn hard-won privacy rights.
   C. We should support a more proactive approach to stu-
      dent mental health problems and improve communi-
      cation between departments.

Formulate an Argument Strategy

The argument that emerges through this outline will build not
only on evidence drawn from sources but also on the writer's
assumptions. Consider the bare-bones logic of the argument:

   Laws protecting student privacy serve a good purpose.
   (*assumption*)

   If properly interpreted and implemented, federal law as
   currently written is sufficient both to protect student privacy and to ensure campus safety. (*support*)

   We should not change federal law to overturn or restrict
   student privacy rights. (*claim*)

The crucial point about which reasonable people will disagree is the *assumption* that laws protecting student privacy
serve a good purpose. Those who wish to restrict the information made available to parents are likely to agree with this
assumption. Those who favor a policy that allows college officials to inform parents of problems without their children's
permission are likely to disagree.

Writers can accept or partially accept an opposing assumption by making a *concession,* in the process establishing

themselves as reasonable and willing to compromise (see the section "Use Concession" in this chapter). David Harrison does exactly this in the following model synthesis when he summarizes the policies of the University of Kentucky. By raising objections to his own position and conceding some validity to them, he blunts the effectiveness of *counterarguments*. Thus, Harrison concedes the absolute requirement for campus safety, but he argues that this requirement can be satisfied as long as campus officials correctly interpret existing federal law and implement proactive procedures aimed at dealing more effectively with troubled students.

The *claim* of the argument about privacy vs. safety is primarily a claim about *policy*, about actions that should (or should not) be taken. An argument can also concern a claim about *facts* (Does X exist? How can we define X? Does X lead to Y?), a claim about *value* (What is X worth?), or a claim about *cause and effect* (Why did X happen?).

The present argument rests to some degree on a dispute about cause and effect. No one disputes that the primary cause of this tragedy was that a disturbed student was not stopped before he killed people. But many have disputed the secondary cause: Did the massacre happen, in part, because federal law prevented officials from sharing crucial information about the disturbed student? Or did it happen, in part, because university officials failed to interpret correctly what they could and could not do under the law? As you read the following paper, observe how these opposing views are woven into the argument.

Draft and Revise Your Synthesis

The final draft of an argument synthesis, based on the outline above, follows. Thesis, transitions, and topic sentences are highlighted; Modern Language Association (MLA) documentation style is used throughout (except in the citing of federal law).

A cautionary note: When writing syntheses, it is all too easy to become careless in properly crediting your sources. Before drafting your paper, always review the section on Avoiding Plagiarism in Chapter 1.

MODEL ARGUMENT SYNTHESIS

Harrison 1

David Harrison
Professor Shanker
Law and Society I
21 February 2011

Balancing Privacy and Safety
in the Wake of Virginia Tech

1   On April 16, 2007, Seung Hui Cho, a mentally ill
student at Virginia Polytechnic Institute, shot to death
32 fellow students and faculty members, and injured 17
others, before killing himself. It was the worst mass shooting in U.S. history, and the fact that it took place on a
college campus lent a special horror to the event. In the
days after the tragedy, several facts about Seung Hui Cho
came to light. According to the official Virginia State Panel
report on the killings, Cho had exhibited signs of mental
disturbance, including "suicidal and homicidal ideations"
dating back to high school. And during Cho's junior year at
Virginia Tech, numerous incidents occurred that provided
clear warnings of Cho's mental instability and violent
impulses (Virginia Tech Review 1). University administrators, faculty, and officials were aware of these incidents but
failed to intervene to prevent the impending tragedy.

2   In the search for answers, attention quickly focused on
federal rules governing student privacy that Virginia Tech
officials said prevented them from communicating effectively with each other or with Cho's parents regarding his
troubles. These rules, the officials argued, prohibit the
sharing of information concerning students' mental

health with parents or other students. The publicity about such restrictions revived an ongoing debate over university policies that balance student privacy against campus safety. In the wake of the Virginia Tech tragedy, the pendulum seems to have swung in favor of safety. In April 2008, Virginia Governor Tim Kaine signed into law a measure requiring colleges to alert parents when dependent students may be a danger to themselves or to others ("Virginia Tech Massacre" 1). Peter Lake, an educator at Stetson University College of Law, predicted that in the wake of Virginia Tech, "people will go in a direction of safety over privacy" (qtd. in Bernstein, "Mother").

3   The shootings at Virginia Tech demonstrate, in the most horrifying way, the need for secure college campuses. Nevertheless, privacy remains a crucial right to most Americans—including college students, many of whom for the first time are exercising their prerogatives as adults. Many students who pose no threat to anyone will, and should, object strenuously to university administrators peering into and making judgments about their private lives. Some might be unwilling to seek professional therapy if they know that the records of their counseling sessions might be released to their parents or to other students. In responding to the Virginia Tech killings, we should resist rolling back federal rules protecting student privacy; for as long as college officials effectively respond to signs of trouble, these rules already provide a workable balance between privacy and public safety.

4   In these days of *Facebook* and reality TV, the notion of privacy rights, particularly for young people, may seem quaint. In fact, a top lawyer for the search engine *Google*

claimed that in the Internet age, young people just don't care about privacy the way they once did (Cohen A17). Whatever the changing views of privacy in a wired world, the issue of student privacy rights is a serious legal matter that must be seen in the context of the student-college relationship. This relationship has its historical roots in the doctrine of *in loco parentis*, Latin for "in the place of the parents." Generally, this doctrine is understood to mean that the college stands in place of the student's parent or guardian. The college therefore has "a duty to protect the safety, morals, and welfare of their students, just as parents are expected to protect their children" (Pollet).

5   Writing of life at the University of Michigan before the 1960s, one historian observes that "*in loco parentis* comprised an elaborate structure of written rules and quiet understandings enforced in the trenches by housemothers [who] governed much of the what, where, when, and whom of students' lives, especially women: what to wear to dinner, what time to be home, where, when, and for how long they might receive visitors" (Tobin).

6   During the 1960s court decisions began to chip away at the doctrine of *in loco parentis*. These rulings illustrate that the students' rights movement during that era was an integral part of a broader contemporary social movement for civil rights and liberties. In *Dixon v. Alabama State Board of Education*, Alabama State College invoked *in loco parentis* to defend its decision to expel six African-American students without due process for participating in a lunchroom counter sit-in. Eventually, a federal appeals court rejected the school's claim to unrestrained power, ruling that students' constitutional rights did not end once they stepped onto campus (Weigel).

7   Students were not just fighting for the right to hold hands in dorm rooms; they were also asserting their rights as the vanguard of a social revolution. As Stetson law professor Robert Bickel notes: "The fall of *in loco parentis* in the 1960s correlated exactly with the rise of student economic power and the rise of student civil rights" (qtd. in Weigel).

8   The students' rights movement received a further boost with the Family Educational Rights and Privacy Act (FERPA), signed into law by President Ford in 1974. FERPA barred schools from releasing educational records—including mental health records—without the student's permission. The Act provides some important exceptions: educational records *can* be released in the case of health and safety emergencies or if the student is declared a dependent on his or her parents' tax returns (*Family*).

9   In the wake of Virginia Tech, however, many observers pointed the finger of blame at federal restrictions on sharing available mental health information. Also held responsible were the school's officials, who admitted knowing of Cho's mental instability but claimed that FERPA prevented them from doing anything about it. The State of Virginia official report on the killings notes as follows:

> University officials . . . explained their failures to communicate with one another or with Cho's parents by noting their belief that such communications are prohibited by the federal laws governing the privacy of health and education records. (Virginia Tech Review 2)

10   Observers were quick to declare the system broken. "Laws Limit Schools Even after Alarms," trumpeted a

Harrison 5

headline in the *Philadelphia Inquirer* (Gammage and
Burling). Commentators attacked federal privacy law,
charging that the pendulum had swung too far away from
campus safety. Judging from this letter to the editor of the
Wall Street Journal, many agreed wholeheartedly: "Parents
have a right to know if their child has a serious problem,
and they need to know the progress of their child's school-
work, especially if they are paying the cost of the education. Anything less than this is criminal" (Guerriero).

11   As part of this public clamor, some schools have enacted policies that effectively curtail student privacy in favor
of campus safety. For example: after Virginia Tech, Cornell
University began assuming that students were dependents
of their parents. Exploiting what the *Wall Street Journal*
termed a "rarely used legal exception" in FERPA allows
Cornell to provide parents with confidential information
without students' permission (Bernstein, "Bucking" A9).

12   Conversely, the Massachusetts Institute of Technology
lies at the opposite end of the spectrum from Cornell in
its staunch defense of student privacy. M.I.T. has stuck to
its position even in the wake of Virginia Tech, demanding
that the mother of a missing M.I.T. student obtain a sub-
poena in order to access his dorm room and e-mail records.
That student was later found dead, an apparent suicide
(Bernstein, "Mother"). Even in the face of lawsuits, M.I.T.
remains committed to its stance. Its Chancellor explained
the school's position this way:

> Privacy is important. . . . Different students will do dif-
> ferent things they absolutely don't want their parents to
> know about. . . . Students expect this kind of safe place

where they can address their difficulties, try out lifestyles, and be independent of their parents (qtd. in
Bernstein, "Mother").

13   One can easily understand how parents would be outraged by the M.I.T. position. No parent would willingly let
his or her child enter an environment where that child's safety
cannot be assured. Just as the first priority for any government is to protect its citizens, the first priority of an educational institution must be to keep its students safe. But does
this responsibility justify rolling back student privacy rights
or returning to a more traditional interpretation of *in loco
parentis* in the relationship between a university and its students? No, for the simple reason that the choice is a false one.

14   As long as federal privacy laws are properly interpreted
and implemented, they do nothing to endanger campus
safety. The problem at Virginia Tech was not the federal
government's policy; it was the university's own practices
based on a faulty interpretation of that policy. The breakdown began with the failure of Virginia Tech officials to
understand federal privacy laws. Interpreted correctly, these
laws would *not* have prohibited officials from notifying
appropriate authorities of Cho's problems. The Virginia
Tech Review Panel report was very clear on this point:
"[F]ederal laws and their state counterparts afford ample
leeway to share information in potentially dangerous situations" (2). FERPA does, in fact, provide for a "health and
safety emergencies" exception; educational records *can* be
released without the student's consent "in connection with
an emergency, [to] appropriate persons if the knowledge of
such information is necessary to protect the health or safety

of the student or other person…" (232g (b) (1) (g–h)). But
Virginia Tech administrators did not invoke this important
exception to FERPA's privacy rules. (Nor did they inform
students of Cho's initial murder of two students, according
to the Department of Education—an action that might have
averted the thirty other murders (Potter)).

15   An editorial in the *Christian Science Monitor* suggested
several other steps that the university could legally have
taken, including informing Cho's parents that he had been
briefly committed to a mental health facility, a fact that was
public information. The editorial concluded, scornfully,
that "federal law, at least, does recognize a balance between
privacy and public safety, even when colleges can't, or
won't" ("Perilous").

16   To be fair, such confusion about FERPA's contingen-
cies appears widespread among college officials. For this
reason, the U.S. Department of Education's revised privacy
regulations, announced in March 2008 and intended to
"clarify" when schools may release student records, are
welcome and necessary. But simply reassuring anxious
university officials that they won't lose federal funds for
revealing confidential student records won't be enough to
ensure campus safety. We need far more effective intervention for troubled students than the kind provided by
Virginia Tech, which the Virginia Tech Review Panel
blasted for its "lack of resources" and "passivity" (2).
Yet effective interventions can be difficult to coordinate,
and the consequences of inaction are sadly familiar. Three
years after the Virginia Tech shootings, a student sued the
University of California Regents because administrators
at UCLA had allegedly failed to address the troubling

behaviors of another student who later slashed and nearly killed her (Gordon).

17   Schools like the University of Kentucky offer a positive example of intervention, demonstrating that colleges can adopt a robust approach to student mental health without infringing on privacy rights. At Kentucky, "threat assessment groups" meet regularly to discuss a "watch list" of troubled students and decide what to do about them (McMurray). These committees emphasize proactiveness and communication—elements that were sorely missing at Virginia Tech. The approach represents a prudent middle ground between the extreme positions of M.I.T. and Cornell.

18   This middle ground takes full account of student privacy rights. For example, the University of Kentucky's director of counseling attends the threat assessment group's meetings but draws a clear line at what information she shares—for instance, whether or not a student has been undergoing counseling. Instead, the group looks for other potential red flags, such as a sharp drop-off in grades or difficulty functioning in the campus environment (McMurray). This open communication between university officials will presumably also help with delicate judgments—whether, for example, a student's violent story written for a creative writing class is an indication of mental instability or simply an early work by the next Stephen King ("Virginia Tech Massacre" 1).

19   The debate over rights to individual privacy versus public safety is sure to follow students into the wider world because that debate is one instance of a larger issue. The Fourth Amendment protects citizens "against unreasonable searches and seizures." But for more than two centuries, what constitutes *unreasonable* has been vigorously

debated in the courts. Such arguments are not likely to end
any time soon—on or off college campuses. Consider the
recent public controversy over the installation of full body
scanners at U.S. airports and intrusive pat-downs of travelers, measures taken by the U.S. Department of Homeland
Security to foil terrorist threats. Predictably, many pro-
tested what they considered an assault on personal privacy,
complaining that the scanners revealed body parts otherwise hidden by clothing and that the pat-downs amounted
to sexual groping. On September 1, 2010, a civil liberties
group even filed a lawsuit to block deployment of the scanners (Electronic). But many others vigorously defended the
Homeland Security measures as essential to ensuring public
safety. According to a *Washington Post*-ABC News poll,
"Nearly two-thirds of Americans support the new full-body
security-screening machines at the country's airports, as
most say they put higher priority on combating terrorism
than protecting personal privacy" (Cohen and Halsey).

20   What happened at Virginia Tech was a tragedy. Few of
us can appreciate the grief of the parents of the shooting victims at Virginia Tech, parents who trusted that their children
would be safe and who were devastated when that faith was
betrayed. To these parents, the words of the M.I.T. chancellor quoted earlier—platitudes about students "try[ing] out
lifestyles" or "address[ing] their difficulties"—must sound
hollow. But we must guard against allowing a few isolated
incidents, however tragic, to restrict the rights of millions
of students, the vast majority of whom graduate college
safely and without incident. Schools must not use
Virginia Tech as a pretext to bring back the bad old days
of resident assistants snooping on the private lives of

students and infringing on their privacy. That step is the first down a slippery slope of dictating morality. Both the federal courts and Congress have rejected that approach and for good reason have established the importance of privacy rights on campus. These rights must be preserved.

21   The Virginia Tech shooting does not demonstrate a failure of current policy, but rather a breakdown in the enforcement of policy. In its wake, universities have undertaken important modifications to their procedures. We should support changes that involve a more proactive approach to student mental health and improvements in communication between departments, such as those at the University of Kentucky. Such measures will not only bring confidential help to the troubled students who need it, they will also improve the safety of the larger college community. At the same time, these measures will preserve hard-won privacy rights on campus.

Works Cited

Bernstein, Elizabeth. "Bucking Privacy Concerns, Cornell Acts as Watchdog." *Wall Street Journal* 27 Dec. 2007: A1+. *LexisNexis*. Web. 10 Feb. 2011.

—. "A Mother Takes On MIT." *Wall Street Journal* 20 Sept. 2007: A1. *LexisNexis*. Web. 10 Feb. 2011.

Cohen, Adam. "One Friend Facebook Hasn't Made Yet: Privacy Rights." *New York Times* 18 Feb. 2008: A1+. *Academic Search Complete*. Web. 9 Feb. 2011.

Cohen, Jon, and Ashley Halsey III. "Poll: Nearly Two-thirds of Americans Support Full-Body Scanners at Airports." *Washington Post*. The Washington Post Co., 23 Nov. 2010. Web. 17 Feb. 2011.

Electronic Privacy Information Center v. Dept. of
    Homeland Security. No. 10-1157. D.C. Cir. of the US.
    Sept 1, 2010. *epic.org.* Electronic Privacy Information
    Center, 1 Sept. 2010. Web. 15 Feb. 2011.

Family Educational Rights and Privacy Act (FERPA). 20
    U.S.C. §1232g (b) (1) (g–h) (2006). Print.

Gammage, Jeff, and Stacy Burling. "Laws Limit Schools
    Even after Alarms." *Philadelphia Inquirer* 19 Apr.
    2007: A1. *Academic Search Complete.* Web.
    10 Feb. 2011.

Gordon, Larry. "Campus Stabbing Victim Sues UC
    Regents." *Los Angeles Times* 8 Dec. 2010. *LexisNexis.*
    Web. 13 Feb. 2011.

Guerriero, Dom. Letter. *Wall Street Journal* 7 Jan. 2008.
    LexisNexis. Web. 11 Feb. 2011.

McMurray, Jeffrey. "Colleges Are Watching Troubled
    Students." *AP Online.* Associated Press, 28 Mar.
    2008. Web. 11 Feb. 2011.

"Perilous Privacy at Virginia Tech." Editorial. *Christian
    Science Monitor* 4 Sept. 2007: 8. *Academic Search
    Complete.* Web. 10 Feb. 2011.

Pollet, Susan J. "Is 'In Loco Parentis' at the College Level
    a Dead Doctrine?" *New York Law Journal* 288 (2002):
    4. Print.

Potter, Dena. "Feds: Va. Tech Broke Law in '07 Shooting
    Response." *Washington Post.* The Washington Post
    Co., 10 Dec. 2010. Web. 12 Feb. 2011.

Tobin, James. "The Day 'In Loco Parentis' Died."
    Michigan Today. U of Michigan, Nov. 2007. Web. 10
    Feb. 2011.

Harrison 12

U.S. Constitution: Fourth Amendment. *Findlaw.com.*
    Thomson Reuters, n.d. Web. 16 Feb. 2011.
"Virginia Tech Massacre Has Altered Campus Mental
    Health Systems." *Los Angeles Times* 14 Apr. 2008:
    A1+. *LexisNexis.* Web. 8 Feb. 2011.
Virginia Tech Review Panel. *Mass Shootings at Virginia
    Tech, April 16, 2007: Report of the Virginia Tech
    Review Panel Presented to Timothy M. Kaine,
    Governor, Commonwealth of Virginia.* Arlington, VA:
    n.p., 2007. Print.
Weigel, David. "Welcome to the Fun-Free University:
    The Return of *In Loco Parentis* Is Killing Student
    Freedom." *Reasononline.* Reason Magazine, Oct.
    2004. Web. 7 Feb. 2011.

The Strategy of the Argument Synthesis

In his argument synthesis, Harrison attempts to support a
claim—one that favors laws protecting student privacy while
at the same time helping to ensure campus safety—by offering
support in the form of facts (what campuses such as the
University of Kentucky are doing, what Virginia Tech officials
did and failed to do) and opinions (testimony of persons on
both sides of the issue). However, because Harrison's claim
rests on an *assumption* about the value of student privacy laws,
its effectiveness depends partially on the extent to which we,
as readers, agree with this assumption. (See our discussion of
assumptions in Chapter 2.) An assumption (sometimes called
a warrant) is a generalization or principle about how the
world works or should work—a fundamental statement of
belief about facts or values. In this case, the underlying assumption is that college students, as emerging adults and as citizens

with civil rights, are entitled to keep their educational records private. Harrison makes this assumption explicit. Though you are under no obligation to do so, stating assumptions explicitly will clarify your arguments to readers.

Assumptions are often deeply rooted in people's psyches, sometimes derived from lifelong experiences and observations and not easily changed, even by the most logical of arguments. People who lose loved ones in incidents such as Virginia Tech, or people who believe that the right to safety of the larger campus community outweighs the right of individual student privacy, are not likely to accept the assumption underlying this paper, nor are they likely to accept the support provided by Harrison. But readers with no firm opinion might well be persuaded and could come to agree with him that existing federal law protecting student privacy is sufficient to protect campus safety, provided that campus officials act responsibly.

A discussion of the model argument's paragraphs, along with the argument strategy for each, follows. Note that the paper devotes one paragraph to developing each section of the outline (see the section "Develop an Organizational Plan" earlier in this chapter). Note also that Harrison avoids plagiarism by the careful attribution and quotation of sources.

- **Paragraph 1:** Harrison summarizes the key events of the Virginia Tech killings and establishes that Cho's mental instability was previously known to university officials.

  Argument strategy: Opening with the bare facts of the massacre, Harrison proceeds to lay the basis for the reaction against privacy rules that will be described in the paragraphs to follow. To some extent, Harrison encourages the reader to share the outrage of many in the general public that university officials failed to act to prevent the killings before they started.

- **Paragraph 2:** Harrison now explains the federal rules governing student privacy and discusses the public backlash against such rules and the new law signed by the governor of Virginia restricting privacy at colleges within the state.

Argument strategy: This paragraph highlights the debate over student privacy—and in particular the sometimes conflicting demands of student privacy and campus safety that will be central to the rest of the paper. Harrison cites both fact (the new Virginia law) and opinion (the quotation by Peter Lake) to develop this paragraph.

- **Paragraph 3:** Harrison further clarifies the two sides of the apparent conflict between privacy and safety, maintaining that both represent important social values but concluding with a thesis that argues for not restricting privacy.

  Argument strategy: For the first time, Harrison reveals his own position on the issue. He starts the paragraph by conceding the need for secure campuses but begins to make the case for privacy (for example, without privacy rules, students might be reluctant to enter therapy). In his thesis he emphasizes that the demands of both privacy and safety can be satisfied because existing federal rules incorporate the necessary balance.

- **Paragraphs 4–7:** These paragraphs constitute the next section of the paper (see outline in "Develop an Organizational Plan" earlier in this chapter), covering the developments in student privacy over the past few decades. Paragraphs 4 and 5 cover the doctrine of *in loco parentis;* paragraph 6 discusses how court decisions like *Dixon v. Alabama State Board of Education* began to erode this doctrine.

  Argument strategy: This section of the paper establishes the situation that existed on college campuses before the 1960s—and that presumably would exist again were privacy laws to be rolled back. By linking the erosion of the *in loco parentis* doctrine to the civil rights struggle, Harrison attempts to bestow upon pre-1960s college students (especially women), who were "parented" by college administrators, something of the *ethos* of African-Americans fighting for full citizenship during the civil rights era. Essentially, Harrison is making an analogy between the two groups—one that readers may or may not accept.

- **Paragraph 8:** This paragraph on FERPA constitutes the final part of the section of the paper dealing with the evolution of student privacy since before the 1960s. Harrison explains what FERPA is and introduces an exception to its privacy rules that will be more fully developed later in the paper.

  Argument strategy: FERPA is the federal law central to the debate over the balance between privacy and safety, so Harrison introduces it here as the culmination of a series of developments that weakened *in loco parentis* and guaranteed a certain level of student privacy. But since Harrison in his thesis argues that federal law on student privacy already establishes a balance between privacy and safety, he ends the paragraph by referring to the "health and safety" exception, an exception that will become important later in his argument.

- **Paragraphs 9–11:** These paragraphs constitute the section of the paper that covers the arguments *against* student privacy. Paragraph 9 discusses public reaction against both FERPA and Virginia Tech officials, who were accused of being more concerned with privacy than with safety. Paragraph 10 cites anti-privacy sentiments expressed in newspapers. Paragraph 11 explains how, in the wake of Virginia Tech, schools like Cornell have enacted new policies restricting student privacy.

  Argument strategy: Harrison sufficiently respects the sentiments of those whose position he opposes to deal at some length with the counterarguments to his thesis. He quotes the official report on the mass shootings to establish that Virginia Tech officials believed that they were acting according to the law. He quotes the writer of an angry letter about parents' right to know without attempting to rebut its arguments. In outlining the newly restrictive Cornell policies on privacy, Harrison also establishes what he considers an extreme reaction to the massacres: essentially gutting student privacy rules. He is therefore setting up one position on the debate that he will later contrast with other positions—those of M.I.T. and the University of Kentucky.

- **Paragraphs 12–16:** These paragraphs constitute the section of the paper devoted to arguments *for* student privacy. Paragraphs 12 and 13 discuss the M.I.T. position on privacy, as expressed by its chancellor. Paragraph 14 refocuses on FERPA and quotes language to demonstrate that existing federal law provides a health and safety exception to the enforcement of privacy rules. Paragraph 15 quotes an editorial supporting this interpretation of FERPA. Paragraph 16 concedes the existence of confusion about federal rules and makes the transition to an argument about the need for more effective action by campus officials to prevent tragedies like the one at Virginia Tech.

  Argument strategy: Because these paragraphs express Harrison's position, as embedded in his thesis, this is the longest segment of the discussion. Paragraphs 12 and 13 discuss the M.I.T. position on student privacy, which (given that school's failure to accommodate even prudent demands for safety) Harrison believes is too extreme. Notice the transition at the end of paragraph 13: conceding that colleges have a responsibility to keep students safe, Harrison poses a question: Does the goal of keeping students safe justify the rolling back of privacy rights? In a pivotal sentence, he responds, "No, for the simple reason that the choice is a false one." Paragraph 14 develops this response and presents the heart of Harrison's argument. Recalling the health and safety exception introduced in paragraph 8, Harrison now explains *why* the choice is false: he quotes the exact language of FERPA to establish that the problem at Virginia Tech was due not to federal law that prevented campus officials from protecting students, but rather to campus officials who *misunderstood* the law.

  Paragraph 15 amplifies Harrison's argument with a reference to an editorial in the *Christian Science Monitor*. Paragraph 16 marks a transition, within this section, to a position (developed in paragraphs 17 and 18) that Harrison believes represents a sensible stance in the debate over campus safety and student privacy.

Harrison bolsters his case by citing here, as elsewhere in the paper, the official report on the Virginia Tech killings. The report, prepared by an expert panel that devoted months to investigating the incident, carries considerable weight as evidence in this argument.

- **Paragraphs 17–18:** These paragraphs continue the arguments in favor of Harrison's position. They focus on new policies in practice at the University of Kentucky that offer a "prudent middle ground" in the debate.

  Argument strategy: Having discussed schools such as Cornell and M.I.T., where the reaction to the Virginia Tech killings was inadequate or unsatisfactory, Harrison now outlines a set of policies and procedures in place at the University of Kentucky since April 2007. Following the transition at the end of paragraph 16 on the need for more effective intervention on the part of campus officials, Harrison explains how Kentucky established a promising form of such intervention: watch lists of troubled students, threat assessment groups, and more open communication among university officials. Thus Harrison positions what is happening at the University of Kentucky—as opposed to rollbacks of federal rules—as the most effective way of preventing future killings like those at Virginia Tech. Kentucky therefore becomes a crucial example for Harrison of how to strike a good balance between the demands of student privacy and campus safety.

- **Paragraphs 19–21:** In his conclusion, Harrison both broadens the context of his discussion about Virginia Tech and reiterates points made in the body of the paper. In paragraph 19, he turns from the shooting to the broader world, suggesting that the tension between the individual's right to privacy and the public's right to safety is not unique to college campuses. In paragraph 20, he agrees that what happened at Virginia Tech was a tragedy but maintains that an isolated incident should not become an excuse for rolling back student privacy rights and bringing back "the bad old days" when campus officials took an active, and intrusive, interest in students' private lives. In paragraph 21, Harrison reiterates the position stated in his thesis: that the problem at Virginia Tech was not a restrictive federal policy that handcuffed administrators but a breakdown in enforcement. He concludes on the hopeful note that new policies established since Virginia Tech will both protect student privacy and improve campus safety.

Argument strategy: The last three paragraphs, the conclusion, provide Harrison with an opportunity both to extend his thinking beyond a single case and to re-emphasize his main points. In paragraph 19, he moves beyond the world of college and broadens the reach of his argument. The final two paragraphs to some degree parallel the structure of the thesis itself. In paragraph 20, Harrison makes a final appeal against rolling back student privacy rights. This appeal parallels the first clause of the thesis ("In responding to the Virginia Tech killings, we should resist rolling back federal rules protecting student privacy"). In paragraph 21, Harrison focuses not on federal law itself but rather on the kind of measures adopted by schools like the University of Kentucky that go beyond mere compliance with federal law—and thereby demonstrate the validity of part two of Harrison's thesis ("As long as college officials effectively respond to signs of trouble, these rules already provide a workable balance between privacy and public safety"). Harrison thus ends a paper on a grim subject with a note that provides some measure of optimism and that attempts to reconcile proponents on both sides of this emotional debate.

Another approach to an argument synthesis based on the same and additional sources could argue (along with some of the sources quoted in the model paper) that safety as a social value should never be outweighed by the right to privacy. Such a position could draw support from other practices in contemporary society—searches at airports, for example—illustrating that most people are willing to give up a certain measure of privacy, as well as convenience, in the interest of the safety of the community. Whatever your approach to a subject, in first *critically examining* the various sources and then *synthesizing* them to support a position about which you feel strongly, you are engaging in the kind of critical thinking that is essential to success in a good deal of academic and professional work.

DEVELOPING AND ORGANIZING THE SUPPORT FOR YOUR ARGUMENTS

Experienced writers seem to have an intuitive sense of how to develop and present supporting evidence for their claims; this sense is developed through much hard work and practice. Less experienced writers wonder what to say first, and having decided on that, wonder what to say next. There is no single method of presentation. But the techniques of even the most experienced writers often boil down to a few tried and tested arrangements.

As we've seen in the model synthesis in this chapter, the key to devising effective arguments is to find and use those kinds of support that most persuasively strengthen your claim. Some writers categorize support into two broad types: *evidence* and *motivational appeals*. Evidence, in the form of facts, statistics, and expert testimony, helps make the appeal to reason. Motivational appeals—appeals grounded in emotion and upon the authority of the speaker—are employed to get people to change their minds, to agree with the writer or speaker, or to decide upon a plan of activity.

Following are the most common strategies for using and organizing support for your claims.

Summarize, Paraphrase, and Quote Supporting Evidence

In most of the papers and reports you will write in college and in the professional world, evidence and motivational appeals derive from your summarizing, paraphrasing, and quoting of material in sources that either have been provided to you or that you have independently researched. For example, in paragraph 9 of the model argument synthesis, Harrison uses a long quotation from the Virginia Tech Review Panel report to make the point that college officials believed they were prohibited by federal privacy law from communicating with one another about disturbed students like Cho. You will find another long quotation later in the synthesis and a number of brief quotations woven into sentences throughout. In addition, you will find summaries and paraphrases. In each case, Harrison is careful to cite the source.

Provide Various Types of Evidence and Motivational Appeals

Keep in mind that you can use appeals to both reason and emotion. The appeal to reason is based on evidence that consists of a combination of *facts* and *expert testimony*. The sources by Tobin and Weigel, for example, offer facts about the evolution over the past few decades of the *in loco parentis* doctrine. Bernstein and McMurray interview college administrators at Cornell, M.I.T., and the University of Kentucky who explain the changing policies at those institutions. The model synthesis makes an appeal to emotion by engaging the reader's self-interest: If campuses are to be made more secure from the acts of mentally disturbed persons, then college officials should take a proactive approach to monitoring and intervention.

Use Climactic Order

Climactic order is the arrangement of examples or evidence in order of anticipated impact on the reader, least to greatest. Organize by climactic order when you plan to offer a number of categories or elements of support for your claim. Recognize that some elements will be more important—and likely more persuasive—than others. The basic principle here is that you should *save the most important evidence for the end* because whatever you say last is what readers are likely to remember best. A secondary principle is that whatever you say first is what they are *next* most likely to remember. Therefore, when you have several reasons to offer in support of your claim, an effective argument strategy is to present the second most important, then one or more additional reasons, and finally the most important reason. Paragraphs 7–11 of the model synthesis do exactly this.

Use Logical or Conventional Order

Using a logical or conventional order involves using as a template a pre-established pattern or plan for arguing your case.

- One common pattern is describing or arguing a *problem/solution*. Using this pattern, you begin with an introduction in which you typically define the problem, perhaps explain its origins, then offer one or more solutions, then conclude.

- Another common pattern presents *two sides of a controversy*. Using this pattern, you introduce the controversy and (in an argument synthesis) your own point of view or claim; then you explain the other side's arguments, providing reasons why your point of view should prevail.

- A third common pattern is *comparison-and-contrast*. This pattern is so important that we will discuss it separately in the next section.

The order in which you present elements of an argument is sometimes dictated by the conventions of the discipline in which you are writing. For example, lab reports and experiments in the sciences and social sciences often follow this pattern: *Opening* or *Introduction, Methods and Materials* (of the experiment or study), *Results, Discussion*. Legal arguments often follow the so-called IRAC format: *Issue, Rule, Application, Conclusion*.

Present and Respond to Counterarguments

When developing arguments on a controversial topic, you can effectively use *counterargument* to help support your claims. When you use counterargument, you present an argument *against* your claim and then show that this argument is weak or flawed. The advantage of this technique is that you demonstrate that you are aware of the other side of the argument and that you are prepared to answer it.

Here is how a counterargument is typically developed:

I. Introduction and claim

II. Main opposing argument

III. Refutation of opposing argument

IV. Main positive argument

Use Concession

Concession is a variation of counterargument. As in counterargument, you present an opposing viewpoint, but instead of dismissing that position, you *concede* that it has some validity and even some appeal, although your own position is the more reasonable one. This concession bolsters your standing as a fair-minded person who is not blind to the virtues of the other side. In the model synthesis, Harrison acknowledges the grief and sense of betrayal of the parents of the students who were killed. He concedes that parents have a right to expect that "the first priority of an educational institution must be to keep its students safe." But he insists that this goal of achieving campus safety can be accomplished without rolling back hard-won privacy rights.

Here is an outline for a typical concession argument:

I. Introduction and claim

II. Important opposing argument

III. Concession that this argument has some validity

IV. Positive argument(s) that acknowledge the counterargument and (possibly) incorporate some elements of it

Sometimes, when you are developing a counterargument or concession argument, you may become convinced of the validity of the opposing point of view and change your own views. Don't be afraid of this happening. Writing is a tool for learning. To change your mind because of new evidence is a sign of flexibility and maturity, and your writing can only be the better for it.

DEVELOPING AND ORGANIZING SUPPORT FOR YOUR ARGUMENTS

- *Summarize, paraphrase, and quote supporting evidence.*
  Draw on the facts, ideas, and language in your sources.

- *Provide various types of evidence and motivational appeal.*
- *Use climactic order.* Save the most important evidence in support of your argument for the *end*, where it will have the most impact. Use the next most important evidence first.
- *Use logical or conventional order.* Use a form of organization appropriate to the topic, such as problem/solution; sides of a controversy; comparison/contrast; or a form of organization appropriate to the academic or professional discipline, such as a report of an experiment or a business plan.
- *Present and respond to counterarguments.* Anticipate and evaluate arguments against your position.
- *Use concession.* Concede that one or more arguments against your position have some validity; re-assert, nonetheless, that your argument is the stronger one.

THE COMPARISON-AND-CONTRAST SYNTHESIS

A particularly important type of argument synthesis is built on patterns of comparison and contrast. Techniques of comparison and contrast enable you to examine two subjects (or sources) in terms of one another. When you compare, you consider *similarities*. When you contrast, you consider *differences*. By comparing and contrasting, you perform a multifaceted analysis that often suggests subtleties that otherwise might not have come to your (or your reader's) attention.

To organize a comparison-and-contrast argument, you must carefully read sources in order to discover *significant criteria for analysis*. A *criterion* is a specific point to which both of your authors refer and about which they may agree or disagree. (For example, in a comparative report on compact cars, criteria for *comparison and contrast* might be road handling, fuel economy, and comfort of ride.) The best criteria are those that allow you not only to account for obvious similarities and differences—those concerning the main aspects of your sources or subjects—but also to plumb deeper, exploring subtle yet significant comparisons and contrasts among details or subcomponents, which you can then relate to your overall thesis.

Note that comparison-and-contrast is frequently not an end in itself but serves some larger purpose. Thus, a comparison-and-contrast synthesis may be a component of a paper that is essentially a critique, an explanatory synthesis, an argument synthesis, or an analysis.

Organizing Comparison-and-Contrast Syntheses

Two basic approaches to organizing a comparison-and-contrast synthesis are organization by *source* and organization by *criteria*.

Organizing by Source or Subject

You can organize a comparative synthesis by first summarizing each of your sources or subjects and then discussing the significant similarities and differences between them. Having read the summaries and become familiar with the distinguishing features of each source, your readers will most likely be able to appreciate the more obvious similarities and differences. In the discussion, your task is to consider both the obvious and the subtle comparisons and contrasts, focusing on the most significant—that is, on those that most clearly support your thesis.

Organization by source or subject works best with passages that can be briefly summarized. If the summary of your source or subject becomes too long, your readers might have forgotten the points you made in the first summary when they are reading the second. A comparison-and-contrast synthesis organized by source or subject might proceed like this:

I. Introduce the paper; lead to thesis.

II. Summarize source/subject A by discussing its significant features.

III. Summarize source/subject B by discussing its significant features.

IV. Discuss in a paragraph (or two) the significant points of comparison and contrast between sources or subjects A and B. Alternatively, begin the comparison-contrast in Section III as you introduce source/subject B.

V. Conclude with a paragraph in which you summarize your points and, perhaps, raise and respond to pertinent questions.

Organizing by Criteria

Instead of summarizing entire sources one at a time with the intention of comparing them later, you could discuss two sources simultaneously, examining the views of each author point by point (criterion by criterion), comparing and contrasting these views in the process. The criterion approach is best used when you have a number of points to discuss or when passages or subjects are long and/or complex. A comparison-and-contrast synthesis organized by criteria might look like this:

I. Introduce the paper; lead to thesis.

II. Criterion 1
   A. Discuss what author #1 says about this point. Or present situation #1 in light of this point.

   B. Discuss what author #2 says about this point, comparing and contrasting #2's treatment of the point with #1's. Or present situation #2 in light of this point and explain its differences from situation #1.

III. Criterion 2
   A. Discuss what author #1 says about this point. Or present situation #1 in light of this point.

   B. Discuss what author #2 says about this point, comparing and contrasting #2's treatment of the point with #1's. Or present situation #2 in light of this point and explain its differences from situation #1.

And so on, proceeding criterion by criterion until you have completed your discussion. Be sure to arrange criteria with a clear method; knowing how the discussion of one criterion leads to the next will ensure smooth transitions throughout your paper. End by summarizing your key points and perhaps raising and responding to pertinent questions.

However you organize your comparison-and-contrast synthesis, keep in mind that comparing and contrasting are not ends in themselves. Your discussion should point to a conclusion, an answer to the question "So what—why bother to compare and contrast in the first place?" If your discussion is part of a larger synthesis, point to and support the larger claim. If you write a stand-alone comparison-and-contrast synthesis, though, you must by the final paragraph answer the "Why bother?" question. The model comparison-and-contrast synthesis that follows does exactly this.

A Case for Comparison-and-Contrast: World War I and World War II

Let's see how the principles of comparison-and-contrast can be applied to a response to a final examination question in a course on modern history. Imagine that having attended classes involving lecture and discussion, and having read excerpts from John Keegan's *The First World War* and Tony Judt's *Postwar: A History of Europe Since 1945*, you were presented with this examination question:

> Based on your reading to date, compare and contrast the two world wars in light of any four or five criteria you think significant. Once you have called careful attention to both similarities and differences, conclude with an observation. What have you learned? What can your comparative analysis teach us?

Comparison-and-Contrast Organized by Criteria

Here is a plan for a response, essentially a comparison-and-contrast synthesis, organized by *criteria* and beginning with the thesis—and the *claim*.

> *Thesis:* In terms of the impact on cities and civilian populations, the military aspects of the two wars in Europe, and their

aftermaths, the differences between World War I and World War II considerably outweigh the similarities.

I. Introduction. World Wars I and II were the most devastating conflicts in history. *Thesis*

II. Summary of main similarities: causes, countries involved, battlegrounds, global scope.

III. First major difference: Physical impact of war.

A. World War I was fought mainly in rural battlegrounds.

B. In World War II cities were destroyed.

IV. Second major difference: Effect on civilians.

A. World War I fighting primarily involved soldiers.

B. World War II involved not only military but also massive noncombatant casualties: civilian populations were displaced, forced into slave labor, and exterminated.

V. Third major difference: Combat operations.

A. World War I, in its long middle phase, was characterized by trench warfare.

B. During the middle phase of World War II, there was no major military action in Nazi-occupied Western Europe.

VI. Fourth major difference: Aftermath.

A. Harsh war terms imposed on defeated Germany contributed significantly to the rise of Hitler and World War II.

B. Victorious allies helped rebuild West Germany after World War II but allowed Soviets to take over Eastern Europe.

VII. Conclusion. Since the end of World War II, wars have been far smaller in scope and destructiveness, and warfare has expanded to involve stateless combatants committed to acts of terror.

The following model exam response, a comparison-and-contrast synthesis organized by criteria, is written according to the preceding plan. (Thesis and topic sentences are highlighted.)

MODEL EXAM RESPONSE

1   World War I (1914–18) and World War II (1939–45) were the most catastrophic and destructive conflicts in human history. For those who believed in the steady but inevitable progress of civilization, it was impossible to imagine that two wars in the first half of the twentieth century could reach levels of barbarity and horror that would outstrip those of any previous era. Historians estimate that more than 22 million people, soldiers and civilians, died in World War I; they estimate that between 40 and 50 million died in World War II. In many ways, these two conflicts were similar: they were fought on many of the same European and Russian battlegrounds, with more or less the same countries on opposing sides. Even many of the same people were involved: Winston Churchill and Adolf Hitler figured in both wars. And the main outcome in each case was the same: total defeat for Germany. However, in terms of the impact on cities and civilian populations, the military aspects of the two wars in Europe, and their aftermaths, the differences between World Wars I and II considerably outweigh the similarities.

2   The similarities are clear enough. In fact, many historians regard World War II as a continuation—after an intermission of about twenty years—of World War I. One of the main causes of each war was Germany's dissatisfaction and frustration with what it perceived as its diminished place in the world. Hitler launched World War II partly out of revenge for Germany's humiliating defeat in World

War I. In each conflict Germany and its allies (the Central Powers in WWI, the Axis in WWII) went to war against France, Great Britain, Russia (the Soviet Union in WWII), and eventually, the United States. Though neither conflict included literally the entire world, the participation of countries not only in Europe but also in the Middle East, the Far East, and the Western hemisphere made both conflicts global in scope. And as indicated earlier, the number of casualties in each war was unprecedented in history, partly because modern technology had enabled the creation of deadlier weapons—including tanks, heavy artillery, and aircraft—than had ever been used in warfare.

3   Despite these similarities, the differences between the two world wars are considerably more significant. One of the most noticeable differences was the physical impact of each war in Europe and in Russia—the western and eastern fronts. The physical destruction of World War I was confined largely to the battlefield. The combat took place almost entirely in the rural areas of Europe and Russia. No major cities were destroyed in the first war; cathedrals, museums, government buildings, urban houses and apartments were left untouched. During the second war, in contrast, almost no city or town of any size emerged unscathed. Rotterdam, Warsaw, London, Minsk, and—when the Allies began their counterattack—almost every major city in Germany and Japan, including Berlin and Tokyo, were flattened. Of course, the physical devastation of the cities created millions of refugees, a phenomenon never experienced in World War I.

4   The fact that World War II was fought in the cities as well as on the battlefields meant that the second war had a much greater impact on civilians than did the first war. With few exceptions, the civilians in Europe during WWI

were not driven from their homes, forced into slave labor, starved, tortured, or systematically exterminated. But all of these crimes happened routinely during WWII. The Nazi occupation of Europe meant that the civilian populations of France, Belgium, Norway, the Netherlands, and other conquered lands, along with the industries, railroads, and farms of these countries, were put into the service of the Third Reich. Millions of people from conquered Europe—those who were not sent directly to the death camps—were forcibly transported to Germany and put to work in support of the war effort.

5   During both wars, the Germans were fighting on two fronts—the western front in Europe and the eastern front in Russia. But while both wars were characterized by intense military activity during their initial and final phases, the middle and longest phases—at least in Europe—differed considerably. The middle phase of the First World War was characterized by trench warfare, a relatively static form of military activity in which fronts seldom moved, or moved only a few hundred yards at a time, even after major battles. By contrast, in the years between the German conquest of most of Europe by early 1941 and the Allied invasion of Normandy in mid-1944, there was no major fighting in Nazi-occupied Western Europe. (The land battles then shifted to North Africa and the Soviet Union.)

6   And of course, the two world wars differed in their aftermaths. The most significant consequence of World War I was that the humiliating and costly war reparations imposed on the defeated Germany by the terms of the 1919 Treaty of Versailles made possible the rise of Hitler and thus led directly to World War II. In contrast, after the end of the Second World War in 1945, the Allies helped rebuild West Germany (the portion of a divided Germany that it

controlled), transformed the new country into a democracy, and helped make it one of the most thriving economies of the world. But perhaps the most significant difference in the aftermath of each war involved Russia. That country, in a considerably weakened state, pulled out of World War I a year before hostilities ended so that it could consolidate its 1917 Revolution. Russia then withdrew into itself and took no significant part in European affairs until the Nazi invasion of the Soviet Union in 1941. In contrast, it was the Red Army in World War II that was most responsible for the crushing defeat of Germany. In recognition of its efforts and of its enormous sacrifices, the Allies allowed the Soviet Union to take control of the countries of Eastern Europe after the war, leading to fifty years of totalitarian rule—and the Cold War.

7   While the two world wars that devastated much of Europe were similar in that, at least according to some historians, they were the same war interrupted by two decades, and similar in that combatants killed more efficiently than armies throughout history ever had, the differences between the wars were significant. In terms of the physical impact of the fighting, the impact on civilians, the action on the battlefield at mid-war, and the aftermaths, World Wars I and II differed in ways that matter to us decades later. The wars in Iraq, Afghanistan, and Bosnia have involved an alliance of nations pitted against single nations; but we have not seen, since the two world wars, grand alliances moving vast armies across continents. The destruction implied by such action is almost unthinkable today. Warfare is changing, and "stateless" combatants like Hamas and Al Qaeda wreak destruction of their own. But we may never again see, one hopes, the devastation that follows when multiple nations on opposing sides of a conflict throw millions of soldiers— and civilians—into harm's way.

The Strategy of the Exam Response

The general strategy of this argument is an organization by *criteria*. The writer argues that although the two world wars exhibited some similarities, the differences between the two conflicts were more significant. Note that the writer's thesis doesn't merely state these significant differences; it also presents them in a way that anticipates both the content and the structure of the response to follow.

In argument terms, the *claim* the writer makes is the conclusion that the two global conflicts were significantly different, if superficially similar. The *assumption* is that key differences and similarities are clarified by employing specific criteria: the impact of the wars upon cities and civilian populations and the consequences of the Allied victories. The *support* comes in the form of historical facts regarding the levels of casualties, the scope of destruction, the theaters of conflict, the events following the conclusions of the wars, and so on.

- **Paragraph 1:** The writer begins by commenting on the unprecedented level of destruction of World Wars I and II and concludes with the thesis summarizing the key similarities and differences.

- **Paragraph 2:** The writer summarizes the key similarities in the two wars: the wars' causes, their combatants, their global scope, and the level of destructiveness made possible by modern weaponry.

- **Paragraph 3:** The writer discusses the first of the key differences: the battlegrounds of World War I were largely rural; the battlegrounds of World War II included cities that were targeted and destroyed.

- **Paragraph 4:** The writer discusses the second of the key differences: the impact on civilians. In World War I, civilians were generally spared from the direct effects of combat; in World War II, civilians were targeted by the Nazis for systematic displacement and destruction.

- **Paragraph 5:** The writer discusses the third key difference: Combat operations during the middle phase of

World War I were characterized by static trench warfare. During World War II, in contrast, there were no major combat operations in Nazi-occupied Western Europe during the middle phase of the conflict.

- **Paragraph 6:** The writer focuses on the fourth key difference: the aftermath of the two wars. After World War I, the victors imposed harsh conditions on a defeated Germany, leading to the rise of Hitler and the Second World War. After World War II, the Allies helped Germany rebuild and thrive. However, the Soviet victory in 1945 led to its postwar domination of Eastern Europe.

- **Paragraph 7:** In the conclusion, the writer sums up the key similarities and differences just covered and makes additional comments about the course of more recent wars since World War II. In this way, the writer responds to the questions posed at the end of the assignment: "What have you learned? What can your comparative analysis teach us?"

Avoid Common Fallacies in Developing and Using Support

In Chapter 2, in the section on critical reading, we considered criteria that, as a reader, you may use for evaluating informative and persuasive writing (see pp. 36–37, 38–49). We discussed how you can assess the accuracy, the significance, and the author's interpretation of the information presented. We also considered the importance in good argument of clearly defined key terms and the pitfalls of emotionally loaded language. Finally, we saw how to recognize such logical fallacies as either/or reasoning, faulty cause-and-effect reasoning, hasty generalization, and false analogy. As a writer, no less than as a critical reader, you need to be aware of these common problems and to avoid them.

Be aware, also, of your responsibility to cite source materials appropriately. When you quote a source, double- and triplecheck that you have done so accurately. When you summarize or paraphrase, take care to use your own language and sentence structures (though you can, of course, also quote within these forms). When you refer to someone else's idea—even if you are not quoting, summarizing, or paraphrasing—give the source credit. By being ethical about the use of sources, you uphold the highest standards of the academic community.

THE EXPLANATORY SYNTHESIS

Some of the papers you write in college will be more or less explanatory (as opposed to argumentative) in nature. An explanation helps readers understand a topic. Writers explain when they divide a subject into its component parts and present them to the reader in a clear and orderly fashion. Explanations may entail descriptions that re-create in words some object, place, emotion, event, sequence of events, or state of affairs. As a student reporter, you may need to explain an event—to relate when, where, and how it took place. In a science lab, you would observe the conditions and results of an experiment and record them for review by others. In a political science course, you might review research on a particular subject—say, the complexities underlying the debate over gay marriage—and then present the results of your research to your professor and the members of your class.

Your job in writing an explanatory synthesis—or in writing the explanatory portion of an argument synthesis—is not to argue a particular point, but rather *to present the facts in a reasonably objective manner*. Explanatory papers, like other academic papers, should be based on a thesis. But the purpose of a thesis in an explanatory paper is less to advance a particular opinion than it is to focus the various facts contained in the paper.

The explanatory synthesis is fairly modest in purpose. It emphasizes the materials in the sources, not the writer's interpretation of them. Because your reader is not always in a position to read your sources, this kind of synthesis, if done well, can be very informative. But the main characteristic of the explanatory synthesis is that it is designed more to *inform* than to *persuade*. As the writer of an explanatory synthesis, you remain for the most part a detached observer.

Model Explanatory Synthesis

Let's demonstrate the difference between an argument synthesis and an explanatory synthesis on the same subject. This is the same kind of demonstration we offered early in this chapter (see section "Types of Synthesis: Explanatory and Argument") in the contrast between a news article and an editorial on the same topic: the nutritional value of cheese. One source is primarily explanatory; the other is strongly argumentative. Following is a new, highly excerpted version of the argument synthesis on balancing privacy rights and safety with the argument components removed and the explanatory components reinforced. The writer is now, in effect, simply reporting on the debate rather than commenting upon it or offering his opinions and recommendations. He is now writing an explanatory synthesis.

Much of the content (including the parts represented by ellipses) remains the same as in the argument synthesis—which illustrates the fact that explanation often plays a pivotal role in making arguments. We highlight the sentences and attributive phrases (such as "officials hope"), as well as the revamped the thesis, that help convert this paper from an argument synthesis to an explanatory synthesis.

EXPLANATORY SYNTHESIS

(Thesis and topic sentences are highlighted.)

Privacy vs. Safety in the Wake of Virginia Tech

1 On April 16, 2007, Seung Hui Cho, a mentally ill student at
Virginia Polytechnic Institute, shot to death 32 fellow
students and faculty members, and injured 17 others,
before killing himself. It was the worst mass shooting in
U.S. history, and the fact that it took place on a college
campus lent a special horror to the event. . . .

---

3   The shootings at Virginia Tech demonstrate, in the most horrifying way, the need for secure college campuses. Nevertheless, privacy remains a crucial right to most Americans—including college students, many of whom for the first time are exercising their prerogatives as adults. Many students who pose no threat to anyone will object strenuously to university administrators peering into and making judgments about their private lives. Some might be unwilling to seek professional therapy if they knew that the records of their counseling sessions might be released to their parents or to other students. As they struggled to understand what had gone wrong at Virginia Tech, college officials, mental health professionals, lawmakers, and others attempted to develop new policies and procedures that would help prevent another such incident and also balance the demands of student privacy and campus safety.

4   In these days of *Facebook* and reality TV, the notion of privacy rights, particularly for young people, may seem quaint. . . .

13   One can easily understand how parents would be outraged by the MIT position. No parent would willingly let his or her child enter an environment where that child's safety cannot be assured. Just as the first priority for any government is to protect its citizens, the first priority of an educational institution must be to keep its students safe. But how, exactly, to keep students safe, college officials concede, is a complicated matter.

14   One of the "key findings" of the Virginia Tech Review Panel was that federal privacy laws, properly interpreted and implemented, do nothing to endanger campus safety. "In reality," the panel concluded, "federal laws and their state counterparts afford ample leeway to share information

in potentially dangerous situations (Virginia Tech Review 2). So the problem at Virginia Tech, according to the panel, was not the federal government's policy; it was the university's own practices based on a faculty interpretation of that policy. The breakdown began with the failure of Virginia Tech officials to understand federal privacy laws. . . .

18 This open communication between university officials presumably will also help with delicate judgments—whether, for example, a student's violent story written for a creative writing class is an indication of mental instability or simply an early work by the next Stephen King ("Virginia Tech Massacre" 1).

19-20 The tragic events at Virginia Tech have spurred renewed debate over the often competing claims of student privacy and campus safety. During the course of this debate universities have undertaken important modifications in their procedures. These new policies involve a more proactive approach to student mental health and improvements in communication between departments, such as those at the University of Kentucky. Such measures, officials hope, will not only bring confidential help to the troubled students who need it, they will also improve the safety of the larger college community. At the same time, they expect that these measures will preserve hard-won privacy rights on campus.

The Strategy of the Explanatory Synthesis

In developing this explanatory synthesis, the writer uses much of the same wording—that is, the same facts and claims—that appears in the argument synthesis. But the writer keeps his own opinions to himself. Note especially the new thesis: the original argument thesis that takes a strong position ("we should resist rolling back federal rules") has been replaced by an explanatory thesis reflecting a more neutral stance ("college officials … and others attempted to develop new policies and procedures"). Note also such attributive phrases as "they expect that," which serve to relocate strongly held views away from the writer and credit them to others. As for the conclusion, note that the emphasis remains on explaining, not on finding fault or giving credit.

SUMMARY

In this chapter we've considered two main types of synthesis: the *argument synthesis* and the *explanatory synthesis*. Although for ease of comprehension we've placed them in separate categories, the types are not mutually exclusive. Both argument syntheses and explanatory syntheses often involve elements of one another. Which format you choose will depend upon your *purpose* and the method that you decide is best suited to achieve that purpose.

If your main purpose is to help your audience understand a particular subject, and in particular to help them understand the essential elements or significance of that subject, then you will be composing an explanatory synthesis. If your main purpose, on the other hand, is to persuade your audience to agree with your viewpoint on a subject, or to change their minds, or to decide upon a particular course of action, then you will be composing an argument synthesis. If one effective technique for making your case is to establish similarities or differences between your subject and another one, then you will compose a comparison-and-contrast synthesis—which may well be only *part* of a larger synthesis.

In planning and drafting these syntheses, you can draw upon a variety of strategies: supporting your claims by summarizing, paraphrasing, and quoting from your sources; and choosing from among formats such as climactic or conventional order, counter-argument, and concession to help you achieve your purpose.

The strategies of synthesis you've practiced in this chapter will be important in composing a research paper, the successful execution of which involves all of the skills of summary, critique, and synthesis that we've discussed so far.

4

Analysis

WHAT IS AN ANALYSIS?

An *analysis* is a type of argument in which you study the parts of something—a physical object, a work of art, a person or group of people, an event, a scientific, economic, or sociological phenomenon—to understand how it works, what it means, or why it might be significant. The writer of an analysis uses an analytical tool: a *principle* or *definition* on the basis of which the subject of study can be divided into parts and examined.

Here are excerpts from two analyses of the movie version of L. Frank Baum's *The Wizard of Oz:*

> At the dawn of adolescence, the very time she should start to distance herself from Aunt Em and Uncle Henry, the surrogate parents who raised her on their Kansas farm, Dorothy Gale experiences a hurtful reawakening of her fear that these loved ones will be rudely ripped from her, especially her Aunt (Em—M for Mother!).

> [*The Wizard of Oz*] was originally written as a political allegory about grass-roots protest. It may seem harder to believe than Emerald City, but the Tin Woodsman is the industrial worker, the Scarecrow [is] the struggling farmer, and the Wizard is the president, who is powerful only as long as he succeeds in deceiving the people.

As these paragraphs suggest, what you discover through analysis depends entirely on the principle or definition you use to make your insights. Is *The Wizard of Oz* the story of a girl's psychological development, or is it a story about politics?

The answer is *both*. In the first example, the psychiatrist Harvey Greenberg applies the principles of his profession and, not surprisingly, sees *The Wizard of Oz* in psychological terms. In the second example, a newspaper reporter applies the political theories of Karl Marx and, again not surprisingly, discovers a story about politics.

Different as they are, these analyses share an important quality: Each is the result of a specific principle or definition used as a tool to divide an object into parts in order to see what it means and how it works. The writer's choice of analytical tool simultaneously creates and limits the possibilities for analysis. Thus, working with the principles of Freud, Harvey Greenberg sees *The Wizard of Oz* in psychological, not political, terms; working with the theories of Karl Marx, Peter Dreier understands the movie in terms of the economic relationships among the characters. It's as if the writer of an analysis who adopts one analytical tool puts on a pair of glasses and sees an object in a specific way. Another writer, using a different tool (and a different pair of glasses), sees the object differently.

WHERE DO WE FIND WRITTEN ANALYSES?

Here are just a few of the types of writing that involve analysis:

Academic Writing

- **Experimental and lab reports** analyze the meaning or implications of the study results in the Discussion section.
- **Research papers** analyze information in sources or apply theories to material being reported.
- **Process analyses** break down the steps or stages involved in completing a process.
- **Literary analyses** examine characterization, plot, imagery, or other elements in works of literature.
- **Essay exams** demonstrate understanding of course material by analyzing data using course concepts.

Workplace Writing

- **Grant proposals** analyze the issues you seek funding for in order to address them.
- **Reviews of the arts** employ dramatic or literary analysis to assess artistic works.
- **Business plans** break down and analyze capital outlays, expenditures, profits, materials, and the like.
- **Medical charts** record analytical thinking and writing in relation to patient symptoms and possible options.
- **Legal briefs** break down and analyze facts of cases and elements of legal precedents and apply legal rulings and precedents to new situations.
- **Case studies** describe and analyze the particulars of a specific medical, social service, advertising, or business case.

You might protest: Are there as many analyses of *The Wizard of Oz* as there are people to read the book or to see the movie? Yes, or at least as many analyses as there are analytical tools. This does not mean that all analyses are equally valid or useful. Each writer must convince the reader using the power of her or his argument. In creating an analytical discussion, the writer must organize a series of related insights using the analytical tool to examine first one part and then another part of the object being studied. To read Harvey Greenberg's essay on *The Wizard of Oz* is to find paragraph after paragraph of related insights— first about Aunt Em, then the Wicked Witch, then Toto, and then the Wizard. All these insights point to Greenberg's single conclusion: that "Dorothy's 'trip' is a marvelous metaphor for the psychological journey every adolescent must make." Without Greenberg's analysis, we would probably not have thought about the movie as a psychological journey. This is precisely the power of an analysis: its ability to reveal objects or events in ways we would not otherwise have considered.

The writer's challenge is to convince readers that (1) the analytical tool being applied is legitimate and well matched to the object being studied; and (2) the analytical tool is being used systematically and insightfully to divide the object into parts and to make a coherent, meaningful statement about these parts and the object as a whole.

HOW TO WRITE ANALYSES

Let's consider a more extended example of analysis, one that approaches excessive TV watching as a type of addiction. This analytical passage illustrates the two defining features of the analysis: a statement of an analytical principle or definition and the use of that principle or definition in closely examining an object, behavior, or event. As you read, try to identify these features.

The Plug-In Drug

Marie Winn

This analysis of television viewing as an addictive behavior appeared originally in Marie Winn's book The Plug-In Drug: Television, Computers, and Family Life (2002). A writer and media critic, Winn has been interested in the effects of television on both individuals and the larger culture. In this passage, she carefully defines the term addiction and then applies it systematically to the behavior under study.

1   The word "addiction" is often used loosely and wryly in conversation. People will refer to themselves as "mystery-book addicts" or "cookie addicts." E. B. White wrote of his annual surge of interest in gardening: "We are hooked and are making an attempt to kick the habit." Yet nobody really believes that reading mysteries or ordering seeds by catalogue is serious enough to be compared with addictions to heroin or alcohol. In these cases the word "addiction" is used jokingly to denote a tendency to overindulge in some pleasurable activity.

2   People often refer to being "hooked on TV." Does this, too, fall into the lighthearted category of cookie eating and other pleasures that people pursue with unusual intensity? Or is there a kind of television viewing that falls into the more serious category of destructive addiction?

3   Not unlike drugs or alcohol, the television experience allows the participant to blot out the real world and enter into a pleasurable and passive mental state. To be sure, other experiences, notably reading, also provide a temporary respite from reality. But it's much easier to stop reading and return to reality than to stop watching television. The entry into another world offered by reading includes an easily accessible return ticket. The entry via television does not. In this way television viewing, for those vulnerable to addiction, is more like drinking or taking drugs—once you start it's hard to stop.

4   Just as alcoholics are only vaguely aware of their addiction, feeling that they control their drinking more than they really do ("I can cut it out any time I want—I just like to have three or four drinks before dinner"), many people overestimate their control over television watching. Even as they put off other activities to spend hour after hour watching television, they feel they could easily resume living in a different, less passive style. But somehow or other while the television set is present in their homes, it just stays on. With television's easy gratifications available, those other activities seem to take too much effort.

5   A heavy viewer (a college English instructor) observes:

> I find television almost irresistible. When the set is on, I cannot ignore it. I can't turn it off. I feel sapped, will-less, enervated. As I reach out to turn off the set, the strength goes out of my arms. So I sit there for hours and hours.

6   Self-confessed television addicts often feel they "ought" to do other things—but the fact that they don't read and don't plant their garden or sew or crochet or play games or have conversations means that those activities are no longer as desirable as television viewing. In a way, the lives of heavy viewers are as unbalanced by their television "habit" as drug addicts' or alcoholics' lives. They are living in a holding pattern, as it were, passing up the activities that lead to growth or development or a sense of accomplishment. This is one reason people talk about their television viewing so ruefully, so apologetically. They are aware that it is an unproductive experience, that by any human measure almost any other endeavor is more worthwhile.

7   It is the adverse effect of television viewing on the lives of so many people that makes it feel like a serious addiction. The television habit distorts the sense of time. It renders other experiences vague and curiously unreal while taking on a greater reality for itself. It weakens relationships by reducing and sometimes eliminating normal opportunities for talking, for communicating.

8   And yet television does not satisfy, else why would the viewer continue to watch hour after hour, day after day? "The measure of health," wrote the psychiatrist Lawrence Kubie, "is flexibility… and especially the freedom to cease when sated." But heavy television viewers can never be sated with their television experiences. These do not provide the true nourishment that satiation requires, and thus they find that they cannot stop watching.

Locate and Apply an Analytic Tool

The general purpose of all analysis is to enhance one's understanding of the subject under consideration. A good analysis provides a valuable—if sometimes unusual or unexpected—point of view, a way of *seeing*, a way of *interpreting* some phenomenon, person, event, policy, or pattern of behavior that otherwise may appear random or unexplainable. How well the analysis achieves its purpose depends upon the suitability to the subject and the precision of the analytical tools selected and upon the skill with which the writer (or speaker) applies these tools. Each reader must determine for her- or himself whether the analysis enhances understanding or—in the opposite case—is merely confusing or irrelevant. To what extent does it enhance your understanding of *The Wizard of Oz* to view the story in psychological terms? In political terms? To what extent does it enhance your understanding of excessive TV watching to view such behavior as an addiction?

When you are faced with writing an analysis, consider these two general strategies:

- Locate an analytic tool—a principle or definition that makes a general statement about the way something works.

- Systematically apply this principle or definition to the subject under consideration.

Let's more fully consider each of these strategies.

Locate an Analytic Tool

In approaching her subject, Marie Winn finds in the definition of "addiction" a useful principle for making sense of the way some people watch TV. The word "addiction," she notes, "is used jokingly to denote a tendency to overindulge in some pleasurable activity." The question she decides to tackle is whether, in the case of watching TV, such overindulgence is harmless, or whether it is destructive, and thus constitutes an addiction.

Make yourself aware, as both writer and reader, of a tool's strengths and limitations. Pose these questions of the analytical principle and definitions you use:

- Are they accurate?
- Are they well accepted?
- Do you accept them?
- How successfully do they account for or throw light upon the phenomenon under consideration?
- What are the arguments against them?
- What are their limitations?

Since every principle of definition used in an analysis is the end product of an argument, you are entitled—even obligated—to challenge it. If the analytical tool is flawed, the analysis that follows from it will necessarily be flawed.

Some, for example, would question whether addiction is a useful concept to apply to television viewing. First, we usually think of addiction as applying only to substances such as alcohol, nicotine, or drugs (whether legal or illegal). Second, many people think that the word "addiction" carries inappropriate moral connotations: we disapprove of addicts and think that they have only themselves to blame for their condition. For a time, the American Psychiatric Association dropped the word "addiction" from its definitive guide to psychological disorders, the *Diagnostic and Statistical Manual of Mental Disorders* (*DSM*), in favor of the more neutral term "dependence." (The latest edition of the *DSM* has returned to the term "addiction.")

On the other hand, "addiction"—also known as "impulse control disorder"— has long been applied to behavior as well as to substances. People are said to be addicted to gambling, to shopping, to eating, to sex, even to hoarding newspapers. The editors of the new *DSM* are likely to add Internet addiction to the list of impulse control disorders. The term even has national implications: many argue that this country must break its "addiction" to oil. Thus, there is considerable precedent for Winn to argue that excessive TV watching constitutes an addiction.

Apply the Analytic Tool

Having suggested that TV watching may be an addiction, Winn uses established psychological criteria* to identify the chief components of addictive behavior. She then applies each one of them to the behavior under consideration. In doing so, she presents her case that TV is a "plug-in drug"; and her readers are free to evaluate the success and persuasiveness of her analysis.

In the body of her analysis, Winn systematically applies the component elements of addiction to TV watching. Winn does this by identifying the major components of addiction and applying them to television watching. Users—

1. turn away from the real world.
2. overestimate how much control they have over their addiction.

---

*For example, the Web site AddictionsandRecovery.org, drawing upon the *Diagnostic and Statistical Manual of Mental Disorders* (DSM) criteria, identifies seven components of substance addiction. A person who answers yes to three of the following questions meets the medical definition of addiction: **Tolerance** (increased use of drugs or alcohol increased over time); **Withdrawal** (adverse physical or emotional reactions to not using); **Difficulty controlling your use** (using more than you would like); **Negative consequences** (using even though use negatively affects mood, self-esteem, health, job, or family); **Neglecting or postponing activities** (putting off or reducing social, recreational, work in order to use); **Spending significant time or emotional energy** (spending significant time obtaining, using, concealing, planning, recovering from, or thinking about use); **Desire to cut down.**

3. lead unbalanced lives and turn away from social activities.

4. develop a distorted sense of time.

5. are never satisfied with their use.

Analysis across the Curriculum

The principle that you select can be a theory as encompassing as the statement that *myths are the enemy of truth.* It can be as modest as the definition of a term such as *addiction* or *comfort.* As you move from one subject area to another, the principles and definitions you use for analysis will change, as these assignments illustrate:

Sociology: Write a paper in which you place yourself in American society by locating both your absolute position and relative rank on each single criterion of social stratification used by Lenski and Lenski. For each criterion, state whether you have attained your social position by yourself or have "inherited" that status from your parents.

Literature: Apply principles of Jungian psychology to Hawthorne's "Young Goodman Brown." In your reading of the story, apply Jung's principles of the *shadow, persona,* and *anima.*

Physics: Use Newton's second law ($F = ma$) to analyze the acceleration of a fixed pulley from which two weights hang: m_1 (.45 kg) and m_2 (.90 kg). Explain in a paragraph the principle of Newton's law and your method of applying it to solve the problem. Assume your reader is not comfortable with mathematical explanations: do not use equations in your paragraph.

Finance: Using Guidford C. Babcock's "Concept of Sustainable Growth" [*Financial Analysis* 26 (May–June 1970): 108–14], analyze the stock price appreciation of the XYZ Corporation, figures for which are attached.

The analytical tools to be applied in these assignments must be appropriate to the discipline. Writing in response to

the sociology assignment, you would use sociological principles developed by Lenski and Lenski. In your literature class,
you would use principles of Jungian psychology; in physics,
Newton's second law; and in finance, a particular writer's
concept of "sustainable growth." But whatever discipline you
are working in, the first part of your analysis will clearly state
which (and whose) principles and definitions you are applying. For audiences unfamiliar with these principles, you will
need to explain them; if you anticipate objections to their use,
you will need to argue that they are legitimate principles capable of helping you conduct the analysis.

GUIDELINES FOR WRITING ANALYSES

Unless you are asked to follow a specialized format,
especially in the sciences or the social sciences, you can
present your analysis as a paper by following the guidelines
below. As you move from one class to another, from
discipline to discipline, the principles and definitions you
use as the basis for your analyses will change, but the following basic components of analysis will remain the same.

- *Create a context for your analysis.* Introduce and summarize
  for readers the object, event, or behavior to be analyzed.
  Present a strong case for why an analysis is needed: Give
  yourself a motivation to write, and give readers a motivation to read. Consider setting out a problem, puzzle,
  or question to be investigated.
- *Locate an analytic tool: a principle or definition that will form
  the basis of your analysis.* Plan to devote an early part of
  your analysis to arguing for the validity of this principle
  or definition if your audience is not likely to understand
  it or if they are likely to think that the principle or definition
  is not valuable.
- *Analyze your topic by applying your selected analytic tool to
  the topic's component elements.* Systematically apply

elements of the analytic tool to parts of the activity or object under study. You can do this by posing specific questions, based on your analytic principle or definition, about the object or phenomenon. Discuss what you find part by part (organized perhaps by question), in clearly defined subsections of the paper.

- *Conclude by stating clearly what is significant about your analysis.* When considering your analytical paper as a whole, what new or interesting insights have you made concerning the object under study? To what extent has your application of the definition or principle helped you to explain how the object works, what it might mean, or why it is significant?

Formulate a Thesis

Like any other thesis, the thesis of an analysis compresses into a single sentence the main idea of your presentation. Some authors omit an explicit thesis statement, preferring to leave the thesis implied. Underlying Winn's analysis, for example, is an implied thesis: "By applying my multipart definition, we can understand television viewing as an addiction." Other authors may take two or perhaps even more sentences to articulate their thesis. But stated or implied, one sentence or more, your thesis must be clearly formulated at least in your own mind if your analysis is to hold together.

The analysis itself, as we have indicated, is a two-part argument. The first part states and establishes your use of a certain principle or definition that serves as your analytic tool. The second part applies specific parts or components of the principle or definition to the topic at hand.

Develop an Organizational Plan

You will benefit enormously in the writing of a first draft if you plan out the logic of your analysis. Turn key elements of your analytical principle or definition into questions, and then develop the paragraph-by-paragraph logic of the paper.

Turning Key Elements of a Principle or a Definition into Questions

Prepare for an analysis by phrasing questions based on the definition or principle you are going to apply, and then directing those questions to the activity or object to be studied. The method is straightforward:

- State as clearly as possible the principle or definition to be applied.
- Divide the principle or definition into its parts.
- Using each part, form a question.

For example, Marie Winn develops a multipart definition of addiction, each part of which is readily turned into a question that she directs at a specific behavior: television viewing. Her analysis of television viewing can be understood as *responses* to each of her analytical questions. Note that in her brief analysis, Winn does not first define addiction and then analyze television viewing. Rather, *as* she defines aspects of addiction, she analyzes television viewing.

Developing the Paragraph-by-Paragraph Logic of Your Paper

The following paragraph from Marie Winn's analysis illustrates the typical logic of a paragraph in an analytical paper:

> Self-confessed television addicts often feel they "ought" to do other things—but the fact that they don't read and don't plant their garden or sew or crochet or play games or have conversations means that those activities are no longer as desirable as television viewing. In a way, the lives of heavy viewers are as unbalanced by their television "habit" as drug addicts' or alcoholics' lives. They are living in a holding pattern, as it were, passing up the activities that lead to growth or development or a sense of accomplishment. This is one reason people talk about

their television viewing so ruefully, so apologetically. They are aware that it is an unproductive experience, that by any human measure almost any other endeavor is more worthwhile.

We see in this paragraph the typical logic of an analysis:

- *The writer introduces a specific analytical tool.* Winn refers to one of the established components of addiction: the addictive behavior crowds out and takes precedence over other, more fruitful activities.

- *The writer applies this analytical tool to the object being examined.* Winn points out that people who spend their time watching television "don't read and don't plant their garden or sew or crochet or play games or have conversations. ... "

- *The writer uses the tool to identify and then examine the significance of some aspect of the subject under discussion.* Having applied the analytic tool to the subject of television viewing, Winn generalizes about the significance of what is revealed: "This is one reason people talk about their television viewing so ruefully, so apologetically. They are aware that it is an unproductive experience, that by any human measure almost any other endeavor is worthwhile."

An analytic paper takes shape when a writer creates a series of such paragraphs, links them with an overall logic, and draws a general conclusion concerning what was learned through the analysis. Here is the logical organization of Marie Winn's analysis:

- *Paragraph 1:* Introduces the word "addiction" and indicates how the term is generally used.

- *Paragraph 2:* Suggests that television watching might be viewed as a "destructive addiction."

- *Paragraph 3:* Discusses the first component of the definition of addiction: an experience that "allows the participant to blot out the real world and enter into a pleasurable and passive mental state." Applies this first component to television viewing.

- *Paragraphs 4 and 5:* Discuss the second component of addiction—the participant has an illusion of control—and apply this to the experience of television viewing.

- *Paragraph 6:* Discusses the third component of addiction—because it requires so much time and emotional energy, the addictive behavior crowds out other, more productive or socially desirable activities—and applies this to the experience of television viewing.

- *Paragraph 7:* Discusses the fourth component of addiction—the negative consequences arising from the behavior—and applies this to the experience of television viewing.

- *Paragraph 8:* Discusses the fifth component of addiction—the participant is never satisfied because the experience is essentially empty—and applies this to the experience of television viewing. Note that in this paragraph, Winn brings in for support a relevant quotation by the psychiatrist Lawrence Kubie.

Draft and Revise Your Analysis

You will usually need at least two drafts to produce a paper that presents your idea clearly. The biggest changes in your paper will typically come between your first and second drafts. No paper that you write, analysis or otherwise, will be complete until you revise and refine your single compelling idea—in the case of analysis, your analytical conclusion about what the object, event, or behavior being examined means or how it is significant. You revise and refine by evaluating your first draft, bringing to it many of the same questions you pose when evaluating any piece of writing:

- Are the facts accurate?
- Are my opinions supported by evidence?
- Are the opinions of others authoritative?
- Are my assumptions clearly stated?

- Are key terms clearly defined?
- Is the presentation logical?
- Are all parts of the presentation well developed?
- Are significant opposing points of view presented?

Address these same questions to the first draft of your analysis, and you will have solid information to guide your revision.

Write an Analysis, Not a Summary

The most common error made in writing analyses—an error that is *fatal* to the form—is to present readers with a summary only. For analyses to succeed, you must *apply* a principle or definition and reach a conclusion about the object, event, or behavior you are examining. By definition, a summary (see chapter 1) includes none of your own conclusions. Summary is naturally a part of analysis; you will need to summarize the object or activity being examined and, depending on the audience's needs, summarize the principle or definition being applied. But in an analysis, you must take the next step and share insights that suggest the meaning or significance of some object, event, or behavior.

Make Your Analysis Systematic

Analyses should give the reader the sense of a systematic, purposeful examination. Marie Winn's analysis illustrates the point: She sets out specific elements of addictive behavior in separate paragraphs and then uses each, within its paragraph, to analyze television viewing. Winn is systematic in her method, and we are never in doubt about her purpose.

Imagine another analysis in which a writer lays out four elements of a definition and then applies only two, without explaining the logic for omitting the others. Or imagine an analysis in which the writer offers a principle for analysis but directs it to only a half or a third of the object being discussed, without providing a rationale for doing so. In both cases, the writer fails to deliver on a promise basic to analyses: Once a principle or definition is presented, it should be thoroughly and systematically applied.

Answer the "So What?" Question

An analysis should make readers *want* to read it. It should give readers a sense of getting to the heart of the matter, that what is important in the object or activity under analysis is being laid bare and discussed in revealing ways. If when rereading the first draft of your analysis, you cannot imagine readers saying, "I never thought of _____ this way," then something may be seriously wrong. Reread closely to determine why the paper might leave readers flat and exhausted, as opposed to feeling that they have gained new and important insights. Closely reexamine your own motivations for writing. Have *you* learned anything significant through the analysis? If not, neither will readers, and they will turn away. If you have gained important insights through your analysis, communicate them clearly. At some point, pull together your related insights and say, in effect, "Here's how it all adds up."

Attribute Sources Appropriately

In an analysis, you often work with just a few sources and apply insights from them to some object or phenomenon you want to understand more thoroughly. Because you are not synthesizing large quantities of data, and because the strength of an analysis derives mostly from *your* application of a principle or definition, the opportunities for not appropriately citing sources are diminished. However, take special care to cite and quote, as necessary, those sources that you draw upon throughout the analysis.

CRITICAL READING FOR ANALYSIS

- *Read to get a sense of the whole in relation to its parts.* Whether you are clarifying for yourself a principle or a definition to be used in an analysis, or you are reading a text that you will analyze, understand how parts function to create the whole. If a definition or principle consists of parts, use them to organize sections of your analysis. If your goal is to analyze a text, be aware of its structure: Note the title and subtitle; identify the main point and subordinate points and where they are located; break the material into sections.

- *Read to discover relationships within the object being analyzed.* Watch for patterns. When you find them, be alert—for they create an occasion to analyze, to use a principle or definition as a guide in discussing what the patterns may mean.

   In fiction, a pattern might involve responses of characters to events or to each other, the recurrence of certain words or phrasings, images, themes, or turns of plot (to name a few).

   In poetry, a pattern might involve rhyme schemes, rhythm, imagery, figurative or literal language, and more.

The challenge to you as a reader is first to see a pattern (perhaps using a guiding principle or definition to do so) and then to locate other instances of that pattern. Reading carefully in this way prepares you to conduct an analysis.

When *Your* Perspective Guides the Analysis

In some cases a writer's analysis of a phenomenon or a work of art may not result from anything as structured as a principle or a definition. It may instead follow from the writer's cultural or personal outlook, perspective, or interests. Imagine reading a story or observing the lines of a new building and being asked to analyze it—based not on someone else's definition or principle, but on your own. Your analysis of the story might largely be determined by your preference for fast pacing; intrepid, resourceful heroes; and pitiless, black-hearted villains. Among the principles you might use in analyzing the building are your admiration for curved exterior surfaces and the imaginative use of glass.

Analyses in this case continue to probe the parts of things to understand how they work and what they mean. And they continue to be carefully structured, examining one part of a phenomenon at a time. The essential purpose of the analysis, to *reveal*, remains unchanged. This goal distinguishes the analysis from the critique, whose main purpose is to *evaluate* and *assess validity*.

An intriguing example of how shifts in personal perspective over time may affect one's analysis of a particular phenomenon is offered by Terri Martin Hekker. In 1977, Hekker wrote an op-ed for the *New York Times* viewing traditional marriage from a perspective very different from that of contemporary feminists, who, she felt, valued self-fulfillment through work more than their roles as traditional housewives:

> I come from a long line of women...who never knew they were unfulfilled. I can't testify that they were happy, but they *were* cheerful.... They took pride in a clean, comfortable home and satisfaction in serving a good meal because no one had explained to them that the only work worth doing is that for which you get paid.

Hekker's view of the importance of what she calls "housewifery"—the role of the traditional American wife and mother—derived from her own personal standards and ideals, which themselves derived from a cultural perspective that she admitted were no longer in fashion in the late 1970s.

Almost thirty years later (2006), Hekker's perspective had dramatically shifted. Her shattering experiences in the wake of her unexpected divorce had changed her view—and as a result, her analysis—of the status, value, and prospects of the traditional wife:

> Like most loyal wives of our generation, we'd contemplated eventual widowhood but never thought we'd end up divorced.... If I had it to do over again, I'd still marry the man I married and

have my children.... But I would have used the years after my youngest started school to further my education. I could have amassed two doctorates using the time and energy I gave myself to charitable and community causes and been better able to support myself.

Hekker's new analysis of the role of the traditional wife derives from her changed perspective, based on her own experience and the similar experiences of a number of her divorced friends.

If you find yourself writing an analysis guided by your own insights, not by someone else's, then you owe your reader a clear explanation of your guiding principles and the definitions by which you will probe the subject under study. Continue using the Guidelines for Writing Analyses, modifying this advice as you think fit to accommodate your own personal outlook, perspective, or interests. Above all, remember to structure your analysis with care. Proceed systematically and emerge with a clear statement about what the subject means, how it works, or why it might be significant.

DEMONSTRATION: ANALYSIS

Linda Shanker wrote the following paper as a first-semester sophomore in response to this assignment from her sociology professor:

Read Robert H. Knapp's "A Psychology of Rumor" in your course anthology. Use some of Knapp's observations about rumor to examine a particular rumor that you have read about in your reading during the first few weeks of this course. Write for readers much like yourself: freshmen or sophomores who have taken one course in sociology. Your object in this paper is to draw upon Knapp to shed light on how the particular rumor you select spread so widely and so rapidly.

MODEL ANALYSIS

Linda Shanker
Social Psychology 1
UCLA
17 November 2010

The Case of the Missing Kidney: An Analysis of Rumor

> Rumor! What evil can surpass her speed?
> In movement she grows mighty, and achieves
> strength and dominion as she swifter flies...
>
> [F]oul, whispering lips, and ears, that catch at all...
> She can cling
> to vile invention and malignant wrong,
> or mingle with her word some tidings true.
> —*Virgil, The Aeneid (Book IV, Ch. 8)*

1   The phenomenon of rumor has been an object of fascination since ancient times. In his epic poem *The Aeneid,* Virgil noted some insidious truths about rumors: they spread quickly—especially in our own day, by means of phones, TV, e-mail, and Twitter; they can grow in strength and come to dominate conversation with vicious lies; and they are often mixed with a small portion of truth, a toxic combination that provides the rumor with some degree of credibility. In more recent years, sociologists and psychologists have studied various aspects of rumors: why they are such a common feature of any society, how they tie in to our individual and group views of the world, how and why they spread, why people believe them, and finally, how they can be prevented and contained.

Shanker 2

2   One of the most important studies is Robert H. Knapp's "A
Psychology of Rumor," published in 1944. Knapp's article
appeared during World War II (during which he was in charge
of rumor control for the Massachusetts Committee of Public
Safety), and many of his examples are drawn from rumors that
sprang up during that conflict; but his analysis of why rumors
form and how they work remains just as relevant today. First,
Knapp defines rumor as an unverified statement offered about
some topic in the hope that others will believe it (22). He proceeds to classify rumors into three basic types: the *pipe-dream
or wish rumor,* based on what we would like to happen; the
bogie rumor, based on our fears and anxieties; and the *wedge-
driving or aggression rumor,* based on "dividing groups and
destroying loyalties" (23–24). He notes that rumors do not
spread randomly through the population, but rather through
certain "sub-groups and factions" who are most susceptible
to believing them. Rumors spread particularly fast, he notes,
when these groups do not trust officials to tell them the truth.
Most important, he maintains, "rumors express the underlying
hopes, fears, and hostilities of the group" (27).

3   Not all rumors gain traction, of course, and Knapp goes
on to outline the qualities that make for successful rumors.
For example, a good rumor must be "short, simple, and
salient." It must be a good story. Qualities that make for a
good story include "a humorous twist...striking and aesthetic
detail...simplification of plot and circumstances...[and]
exaggeration" (29). Knapp explains how the same rumor
can take various forms, each individually
suited to the groups among which it is circulating: "[n]
ames, numbers, and places are typically the most unstable

Shanker 3

components of any rumor." Successful rumors adapt themselves to the particular circumstances, anxieties, prejudices of the group, and the details change according to the "tide of current swings in public opinion and interest" (30).

4   Knapp's insights are valuable in helping us to understand why some contemporary rumors have been so frightening and yet so effective, for instance, the rumor of the missing kidney. One version of this story, current in 1992, is recounted by Robert Dingwall, a sociologist at the University of Nottingham in England:

> A woman friend of another customer had a 17-year-old son who went to a night club in Nottingham, called the Black Orchid, one Friday evening. He did not come home, so she called the police, who were not very interested because they thought that he had probably picked up a girl and gone home with her. He did not come back all weekend, but rang his mother from a call box on Monday, saying he was unwell. She drove out to pick him up and found him slumped on the floor of the call box. He said that he had passed out after a drink in the club and remembered nothing of the weekend. There was a neat, fresh scar on his abdomen. She took him to the Queen's Medical Centre, the main emergency hospital in the city, where the doctors found that he had had a kidney removed. The police were called again and showed much more interest. A senior officer spoke to the mother and said that there was a secret surveillance operation going on in this club and others in the same regional chain in other East Midlands cities because they had had several cases of the same kind and they thought that the organs were being removed for sale by an Asian surgeon. (181)

5   It is not clear where this rumor originated, though at
around this time the missing kidney story had served as the
basis of a *Law and Order* episode in 1992 and a Hollywood
movie, *The Harvest,* released in 1992. In any event, within
a few months the rumor had spread throughout Britain,
with the name of the night club and other details varying
according to the city where it was circulating. The following
year, the story was transplanted to Mexico; a year later it
was set in India. In the Indian version, the operation was
performed on an English woman traveling alone who went
to a New Delhi hospital to have an appendectomy. Upon
returning to England, she still felt ill, and after she was
hospitalized, it was discovered that her appendix was still
there but that her kidney had been removed. In subsequent
years the rumor spread to the United States, with versions
of the story set in Philadelphia, New Orleans, Houston,
and Las Vegas. In 1997, the following message, addressed
"Dear Friends," was posted on an Internet message board:

> I wish to warn you about a new crime ring that is targeting
> business travelers. This ring is well organized, well funded,
> has very skilled personnel, and is currently in most major
> cities and recently very active in New Orleans. The crime
> begins when a business traveler goes to a lounge for a
> drink at the end of the work day. A person in the bar walks
> up as they sit alone and offers to buy them a drink. The last
> thing the traveler remembers until they wake up in a hotel
> room bath tub, their body submerged to their neck in ice, is
> sipping that drink. There is a note taped to the wall instruct-
> ing them not to move and to call 911. A phone is on a small
> table next to the bathtub for them to call. The business

traveler calls 911 who have become quite familiar with this crime. The business traveler is instructed by the 911 operator to very slowly and carefully reach behind them and feel if there is a tube protruding from their lower back. The business traveler finds the tube and answers, "Yes." The 911 operator tells them to remain still, having already sent paramedics to help. The operator knows that both of the business traveler's kidneys have been harvested. This is not a scam or out of a science fiction novel, it is real. It is documented and confirmable. If you travel or someone close to you travels, please be careful ("You've Got to Be").

Subsequent posts on this message board supposedly confirmed this story ("Sadly, this is very true"), adding different details.

6   Is there any truth to this rumor? None, whatsoever— not in any of its forms. Police and other authorities in various cities have posted strenuous denials of the story in the newspapers, on official Web sites, and in internal correspondence, as have The National Business Travel Association, the American Gem Trade Association, and the Sherwin Williams Co. ("'Stolen' Kidney Myth Circulating"). As reported in the rumor-reporting website Snopes.com, "the National Kidney Foundation has asked any individual who claims to have had his or her kidneys illegally removed to step forward and contact them. So far no one's showed up." The persistence and power of the missing kidney rumor can be more fully understood if we apply four of Knapp's principles of rumor formation and circulation to this particular urban legend: his notion of

Shanker 6

the "bogie"; the "striking" details that help authenticate
a "good story" and that change as the rumor migrates to
different populations; the ways a rumor can ride swings of
public opinion; and the mingling of falsehood with truth.

7   The kidney rumor is first and foremost the perfect example
of Knapp's bogie rumor, the rumor that draws its power from
our fears and anxieties. One source of anxiety is being alone in
a strange place. (Recall the scary folk tales about children lost
in the forest, soon to encounter a witch.) These dreaded kidney
removals almost always occur when the victim is away from
home, out of town or even out of the country. Most of us enjoy
traveling, but we may also feel somewhat uneasy in unfamiliar
cities. We're not comfortably on our own turf, so we don't
quite know our way around; we don't know what to expect of
the local population; we don't feel entirely safe, or at least, we
feel that some of the locals may resent us and take advantage
of us. We can relate to the 17-year-old in the Nottingham
nightclub, to the young English woman alone in New Delhi, to
the business traveler having a drink in a New Orleans lounge.

8   Of course, our worry about being alone in an unfamiliar
city is nothing compared to our anxiety about being cut
open. Even under the best of circumstances (such as to save
our lives), no one looks forward to surgery. The prospect
of being drugged, taken to an unknown facility, and having
members of a crime ring remove one of our organs without
our knowledge or consent—as apparently happened to the
various subjects of this rumor—would be our worst night-
mare. It's little wonder that this particular "bogie" man has
such a powerful grip on our hearts.

9   Our anxiety about the terrible things that may happen
to us in a strange place may be heightened because of the
fear that our fate is just punishment for the bad things that
we have done. In the Nottingham version of the rumor, the
victim "had probably picked up a girl and gone home with
her" (Dingwall 181). Another version of the story features
"an older man picked up by an attractive woman" (Dingwall
182). Still another version of the story is set in Las Vegas,
"Sin City, the place where Bad Things Happen to the Unwary
(especially the 'unwary' who were seen as deservedly having
brought it upon themselves, married men intent upon getting
up to some play-for-pay hanky panky" ("You've Got to Be").
As Dingwall notes of this anxiety about a deserved fate, "[t]
he moral is obvious: young people ought to be careful about
night clubs, or more generally, about any activity which takes
them out of a circle of family and friends" (183).

10   In addition to being a classic bogie rumor, Knapp would
suggest that the missing kidney rumor persists because its
"striking and aesthetic detail[s]," while false, have the ring
of truth and vary from one version to another, making for
a "good story" wherever the rumor spreads. Notice that the
story includes the particular names of the bar or nightclub,
the medical facility, the hotel; it describes the size and
shape of the scar; and it summarizes the instructions of
the 911 operator to see if there is a tube protruding from
the victim's back. (The detail about the bathtub full of ice
and the advice to "call 911" was added to the story around
1995.) As Knapp observes, "[n]ames, numbers, and places
are typically the most unstable components of any rumor"
(30), and so the particular cities in which the

Shanker 8

kidney operations are alleged to have been performed, as
well as the particular locations within those cities, changed
as the rumor spread. Another changing detail concerns the
chief villains of this story. Knapp notes that rumors adapt
themselves to the particular anxieties and prejudices of the
group. Many groups hate or distrust foreigners and so we
find different ethnic or racial "villains" named in different
cities. In the Nottingham version of the story, the operation
is performed by an "Asian surgeon." The English woman's
kidney was removed by an Indian doctor. In another version of the story, a Kurdish victim of the kidney operation
was lured to Britain "with the promise of a job by a Turkish
businessman" ("You've Got to Be").

11   Third, Knapp observes that successful rumors "ride
the tide of current swings in public opinion and interest"
(30). From news reports as well as medical and police TV
dramas, many people are aware that there is a great demand
for organ transplants and that such demand, combined with
a short supply, has given rise to a black market for illegally
obtained organs. When we combine this awareness with
stories that appear to provide convincing detail about the
medical procedure involved (the "neat fresh scar," the
tube, the name of the hospital), it is not surprising that
many people accept this rumor as truth without question.
One Internet correspondent, who affirmed that "Yes, this
does happen" (her sister-in-law supposedly worked with a
woman whose son's neighbor was a victim of the operation), noted that the only "good" thing about this situation
was that those who performed the procedure were medically
trained, used sterile equipment, made "exact and

clean" incisions ("You've Got to Be"), and in general took measures to avoid complications that might lead to the death of the patient.

12   Finally, this rumor gains credibility because, as Virgil noted, rumor "mingle[s] with her word some tidings true." Although no documented case has turned up of a kidney being removed without the victim's knowledge and consent, there have been cases of people lured into selling their kidneys and later filing charges because they came to regret their decisions or were unhappy with the size of their payment ("You Got to Be").

13   Rumors can destroy reputations, foster distrust of government and other social institutions, and create fear and anxiety about perceived threats from particular groups of outsiders. Writing in the 1940s about rumors hatched during the war years, Knapp developed a powerful theory that helps us understand the persistence of rumors sixty years later. The rumor of the missing kidney, like any rumor, functions much like a mirror held up to society: it reveals anxiety and susceptibility to made-up but seemingly plausible "facts" related to contemporary social concerns. By helping us to understand the deeper structure of rumors, Knapp's theories can help free us from the "domination" and the "Foul, whispering lips" that Virgil observed so accurately 2,000 years ago.

Works Cited

Dingwall, Robert. "Contemporary Legends, Rumors, and Collective Behavior: Some Neglected Resources for Medical Technology." *Sociology of Health and Illness* 23.2 (2001): 180–202. Print.

Shanker 10

Knapp, Robert H. "A Psychology of Rumor." *Public Opinion Quarterly* 8.1 (1944): 22–37. Print.

"'Stolen' Kidney Myth Circulating: Organ Donation Hurt by Story of Kidney Heist." *UNOS.* United Network for Organ Sharing Newsroom Archive, 20 Aug. 1999. Web. 13 June 2010.

Virgil. *The Aeneid.* Trans. Theodore C. Williams. Perseus 4.0. *Perseus Digital Library.* Web. 17 Oct. 2010.

"You've Got to Be Kidneying." *Snopes.com.* Snopes, 12 Mar. 2008. Web. 12 June 2010.

The Strategy of the Analysis

- Paragraph 1 creates a context for the analysis by introducing the phenomenon of rumor, indicating that it has been an object of fascination and study from ancient times (the poet Virgil is quoted) to the present.

- Paragraphs 2 and 3 introduce the key principle that will be used to analyze the selected rumor, as explained by Robert H. Knapp in his article "A Psychology of Rumor." The principle includes Knapp's definition of rumor, his classification of rumors into three types, and the qualities that make for a successful rumor.

- Paragraph 4 begins by indicating how Knapp's principles can be used to help us understand how rumor works, and then presents one particular manifestation of the rumor to be analyzed, the rumor of the missing kidney. Much of the paragraph consists of an extended quotation describing one of the original versions of the rumor, set in Nottingham, England.

- Paragraph 5 describes how the missing kidney rumor metamorphosed and spread, first throughout England,

and then to other countries, including Mexico, India, and the United States. A second extended quotation describes a version of the rumor set in New Orleans.

- Paragraph 6 explains that the missing kidney rumor has no factual basis, but that its persistence and power can be accounted for by applying Knapp's principles. The final sentence of this paragraph is the thesis of the analysis.

- Paragraph 7 applies the first of Knapp's principles to the missing kidney rumor: it is a bogie rumor that "draws its power from our fears and anxieties." One such fear is that of being alone in an unfamiliar environment.

- Paragraph 8 continues to apply Knapp's principle of the bogie rumor, this time focusing on our fears about being unwillingly operated upon.

- Paragraph 9 discusses another aspect of the bogie rumor, the fear that what happens to us is a form of punishment for our own poor choices or immoral actions.

- Paragraph 10 deals with a second of Knapp's principles, that the "facts" in rumors are constantly changing: names, places, and other details change as the rumor spreads from one city to another, but the reference to specific details lends the rumor a veneer of authenticity.

- Paragraph 11 deals with a third of Knapp's principles: that successful rumors are often based on topics of current public interest—in this case, organ transplants and that, once again, a surface aura of facts makes the rumor appear credible.

- Paragraph 12 returns to Virgil (cited in paragraph 1), who notes that successful rumors also appear credible because they often mix truth with fiction.

- Paragraph 13, concluding the analysis, indicates why it is important to analyze rumor: shedding light on how and why rumors like this one spread may help us to counteract rumors' destructive effects.

Credits

Index

MLA Documentation

QUICK INDEX: MLA Documentation Basic

MLA In-text Citations in Brief

When referring to a source, use parentheses to enclose a page number reference. Include the author's name if you do not mention it in your sentence.

> From the beginning, the AIDS test has been "mired in controversy" (Bayer 101).

Or, if you name the author in the sentence:

> Bayer claims the AIDS test has been "mired in controversy" (101).

MLA Works Cited List in Brief

At the end of the paper, on a separate page titled "Works Cited," alphabetize each cited source by author's last name. Provide full bibliographic information, as shown. State how you accessed the source, via print, Web, or downloaded digital file. As appropriate, precede "Web" with a database name (e.g., *LexisNexis*) or the title of a Web site and a publisher.Follow "Web" with your date of access. Note the use of punctuation and italics.

In MLA style, the medium by which you access a source (print, Web, database, download) determines its Works Cited format.

MAGAZINE OR NEWSPAPER ARTICLE

Article accessed via print magazine or newspaper
> Packer, George. "The Choice." *New Yorker* 28 Jan. 2008: 28–35. Print.
>
> Warner, Judith. "Goodbye to All This." *New York Times* 18 Dec. 2009, late ed.: A27. Print.

Article (version exists in print) accessed via downloaded file
> Packer, George. "The Choice." *New Yorker* 28 Jan. 2008: 28–35. AZW file.
>
> Warner, Judith. "Goodbye to All This." *New York Times* 18 Dec. 2009, late ed.: A27. PDF file.

Article (version exists in print) accessed via database
> Packer, George. "The Choice." *New Yorker* 28 Jan. 2008: 28–35. *Academic Search Premier*. Web. 12 Mar. 2010.

Warner, Judith. "Goodbye to All This." *New York Times* 18 Dec. 2009, late ed.: A27. *LexisNexis.* Web. 14 Jan. 2010.

Article (version exists in print) accessed via Web

Packer, George. "The Choice." *New Yorker.com.* CondéNet, 28 Jan. 2008. Web. 12 Mar. 2010.

Warner, Judith. "Goodbye to All This." *New York Times.* New York Times, 18 Dec. 2009. Web. 14 Jan. 2010.

SCHOLARLY ARTICLE

Scholarly article accessed via print journal

Ivanenko, Anna, and Clifford Massie. "Assessment and Management of Sleep Disorders in Children." *Psychiatric Times* 23.11 (2006): 90–95. Print.

Scholarly article (version exists in print) accessed via downloaded file

Ivanenko, Anna, and Clifford Massie. "Assessment and Management of Sleep Disorders in Children." *Psychiatric Times* 23.11 (2006): 90–95. PDF file.

Scholarly article (version exists in print) accessed via database

Ivanenko, Anna, and Clifford Massie. "Assessment and Management of Sleep Disorders in Children." *Psychiatric Times* 23.11 (2006): 90–95. *Academic OneFile.* Web. 3 Nov. 2010.

Scholarly article (version exists in print) accessed via Web

Ivanenko, Anna, and Clifford Massie. "Assessment and Management of Sleep Disorders in Children." *Psychiatric Times.* United Business Media, 1 Oct. 2006. Web. 3 Nov. 2010.

Scholarly article from an e-journal that has no print equivalent

Blackwood, Jothany. "Coaching Educational Leaders." *Academic Leadership: The Online Journal* 7.3 (2009): n. pag. Web. 2 Feb. 2010.

BOOK

Book accessed via print

James, William. *The Varieties of Religious Experience: A Study in Human Nature; Being the Gifford Lectures on Natural Religion Delivered at Edinburgh in 1901–1902.* New York: Longmans, 1902. Print.

Book (version exists in print) accessed via downloaded file
    James, William. *The Varieties of Religious Experience: A Study
        in Human Nature; Being the Gifford Lectures on Natural
        Religion Delivered at Edinburgh in 1901–1902.* New York:
        Longmans, 1902. MOBI file.

Book (version exists in print) accessed via Web or database
    James, William. *The Varieties of Religious Experience: A Study in
        Human Nature; Being the Gifford Lectures on Natural Religion
        Delivered at Edinburgh in 1901–1902.* New York: Longmans,
        1902. *U. of Virginia Etext Center.* Web. 12 Jan. 2010.
    James, William. *The Varieties of Religious Experience: A Study in
        Human Nature; Being the Gifford Lectures on Natural Religion
        Delivered at Edinburgh in 1901–1902.* New York: Longmans,
        1902. *ACLS Humanities E-Book.* Web. 12 Mar. 2010.

Online book that has no print equivalent
    Langer, Maria. *Mastering Microsoft Word. Designprovideo.com.*
        Nonlinear Educating, 2009. Web. 23 Jan. 2010.

Web-Only Publication (Content Created for and Published on
the Web)
Home page
    Boucher, Marc, ed. Home page. The Space Elevator *Reference.*
    Spaceelevator.com. SpaceRef Interactive, 2009. Web. 17
    Dec. 2009.

Web-based article on a larger site
    Landau, Elizabeth. "Stem Cell Therapies for Hearts Inching
        Closer to Wide Use." *CNN.com.* Cable News Network, 18
        Dec. 2009. Web. 14 Jan. 2010.
    White, Veronica. "Gian Lorenzo Bernini." *Heilbrunn Timeline of
        Art History.* Metropolitan Museum of Art, New York, 2009.
        Web. 18 Mar. 2010.

Blog
    Lubber, Mindy. "The Climate Treaty Announcement." *Climate
        Experts' Forum—Copenhagen.* Financial Times, 19 Dec.
        2009. Web. 22 Dec. 2009.

APA, CMS, AND CSE DOCUMENTATION

QUICK INDEX: APA Documentation Basic

APA In-Text Citations in Brief

When quoting or paraphrasing, place a parenthetical citation in your sentence that includes the author, publication year, and page or paragraph number.

Direct quotation, author and publication year not mentioned in sentence
Research suggests that punishing a child "promotes only momentary compliance" (Berk & Ellis, 2002, p. 383).

Paraphrase, author and year mentioned in the sentence
Berk and Ellis (2002) suggest that punishment may be ineffective (p. 383).

Direct quotation from Internet source
Others have noted a rise in "problems that mimic dysfunctional behaviors" (Spivek, Jones, & Connelly, 2006, Introduction section, para. 3).

APA REFERENCES LIST IN BRIEF

On a separate, concluding page titled "References," alphabetize sources by author, providing full bibliographic information for each.

ARTICLE FROM A JOURNAL

Conclude your entry with the digital object identifier—the article's unique reference number. When a DOI is not available and you have located the article on the Web, conclude with *Retrieved from* and the URL of the home page. For articles located through a database such as *LexisNexis*, do not list the database in your entry.

Article (with volume and issue numbers) located via print or database
Ivanenko, A., & Massie, C. (2006). Assessment and management of sleep disorders in children. *Psychiatric Times, 23*(11), 90–95.

Article (with DOI and volume number) located via print or database
Jones, K. L. (1986). Fetal alcohol syndrome. *Pediatrics in Review, 8,* 122–126. doi:10.1542/10.1542/pir.8-4-122

Article located via Web

>Ivanenko, A., & Massie, C. (2006). Assessment and management
>of sleep disorders in children. *Psychiatric Times, 23*(11),
>90–95. Retrieved from http://www.psychiatrictimes.com

ARTICLE FROM A MAGAZINE

Article (with volume and issue numbers) located via print or database

>Landi, A. (2010, January). Is beauty in the brain of the beholder?
>*ARTnews, 109*(1), 19–21.

Article located via Web

>Landi, A. (2010, January). Is beauty in the brain of the beholder?
>*ARTnews, 109*(1). Retrieved from http://www.artnews.com

ARTICLE FROM A NEWSPAPER

Article located via print or database

>Wakabayashi, D. (2010, January 7). Sony pins future on a 3-D
>revival. *The Wall Street Journal,* pp. Al, A14.

Article located via Web

>Wakabayashi, D. (2010, January 7). Sony pins future on a 3-D
>revival. *The Wall Street Journal.* Retrieved from
>http://www.wsj.com

BOOK

Book located via print

>Mansfield, R. S., & Busse, T. V. (1981). *The psychology of
>creativity and discovery: Scientists and their work.* Chicago,
>IL: Nelson-Hall.

Book located via Web

>Freud, S. (1920). *Dream psychology: Psychoanalysis for
>beginners* (M. D. Elder, Trans.). Retrieved from
>http://www.gutenberg.org

Selection from an edited book

>Halberstam, D. (2002). Who we are. In S. J. Gould (Ed.), *The
>best American essays 2002* (pp. 124–136). New York, NY:
>Houghton Mifflin.

Later edition

>Samuelson, P., & Nordhaus, W. D. (2005). *Economics* (18th ed.).
>Boston, MA: McGraw-Hill Irwin.

CHECKLIST FOR WRITING SUMMARIES (CHAPTER 1)

- **Read the passage carefully.** Determine its structure. Identify the author's purpose in writing.
- **Reread.** *Label* each section or stage of thought. *Highlight* key ideas and terms.
- **Write one-sentence summaries** of each stage of thought.
- **Write a thesis:** a one- or two-sentence summary of the entire passage.
- **Write the first draft** of your summary.
- **Check your summary** against the original passage.
- **Revise** your summary.

CHECKLIST FOR WRITING CRITIQUES (CHAPTER 2)

- **Introduce** both the passage being critiqued and the author.
- **Summarize** the author's main points, making sure to state the author's purpose for writing.
- **Evaluate** the validity of the presentation.
- **Respond** to the presentation: agree and/or disagree.
- **Conclude** with your overall assessment.

CHECKLIST FOR WRITING SYNTHESES (CHAPTER 3)

- **Consider your purpose in writing.**
- **Select and carefully read your sources,** according to your purpose.
- **Take notes as you read.**
- **Formulate a thesis.**
- **Decide how you will use your source material.**
- **Develop an organizational plan,** according to your thesis.
- **Draft the topic sentences for the main sections.**
- **Write the first draft** of your synthesis, following your organizational plan.
- **Document your sources.**
- **Revise your synthesis,** inserting trnsitional words and phrases where necessary.

CHECKLIST FOR WRITING ANALYSES (CHAPTER 4)

- **Summarize** the object, event, or behaviour to be analyzed.
- **Introduce and summarize** the key definition or principle that will form the basis of your analysis.
- **Analyze your topic:** Systematically apply elements of this definition or principle to parts of the activity or object under study.
- **Conclude** by stating clearly what is significant about your analysis. Having worked with a definition or principle, what new or interesting insights have you made?